THE
HOLY SPIRIT
IN
YOUR LIFE

A SYSTEMATIC APPROACH TO A
VIBRANT RELATIONSHIP

THE
HOLY SPIRIT
IN
YOUR LIFE

A SYSTEMATIC APPROACH TO A
VIBRANT RELATIONSHIP

by

George M. Flattery, ED.D.

Network211
Springfield, Missouri
www.network211.com

Network211 (GMF) Edition
Springfield, MO USA
www.network211.com

THE HOLY SPIRIT IN YOUR LIFE:
A SYSTEMATIC APPROACH TO A VIBRANT RELATIONSHIP

ISBN: Network211 (GMF) Paperback Edition: 978-0-9851788-1-9

CONTENTS

INTRODUCTION

Everyone who believes in Christ has the awesome privilege of being a son of our Triune God. All three Persons of the Godhead are involved in making a way for us to be God's sons. The apostle Paul said, "Through Him [Christ] we both [Jews and Gentiles] have our access in one Spirit to the Father" (Eph. 2:18). God gave His Son to redeem us from our sins; the Son did His redemptive work, and the Holy Spirit exalts the Son. Because of all this, we are in Christ and are members of the body of Christ. Although I will deal to some extent with the roles of all three Persons in connection with us as sons of God, my primary focus in this book is on the Holy Spirit and our relationship with Him.

The Main Point

Since 1973, I have been studying all the Scriptures in the Bible that mention the Holy Spirit. Some time ago, I was having a conversation with a friend about these studies. He asked me, "What is the main point that you have learned from your studies?" When you study a subject through the entire Bible, you cover many topics, points of agreement, controversies, and applications of truth. This is true of the doctrine of the Holy Spirit as well as other subjects. However, my goal always has been to focus on our relationship to the Holy Spirit as believers. With this in mind, the main point that I have learned is that our relationship with the Spirit involves all aspects of our lives. His presence and work in and through us has an impact on all that we are and do. As a result, any specific aspect of the doctrine of the Spirit has to be seen within the context of all that He does. Therefore, my work in this book is devoted to presenting the broad scope of the Spirit's relationship to us. My discussion of specific topics takes place within this larger framework.

Inductive Basis

In order to understand the full scope of the Spirit's work, it is important to study the work of the Spirit throughout the Bible. Taking this approach, my work may be described as an inductive study of the relevant biblical data. Based on these studies, I have written *A Biblical Theology of the Holy Spirit* in three volumes. A fourth volume, dealing with contemporary issues, was written by other scholars to complete the four-volume set. We have covered the entire Bible because it is all instructive for us. The entire series has been published.

This book is based on the three volumes that I wrote, consisting of over 1,000 pages and a considerable amount of exegesis. Hundreds of resources were researched in preparing those volumes. Different points of view on many passages are included in the discussions, and many excellent works from various church backgrounds are cited and noted in the footnotes. Hopefully, this will contribute to our understanding of the views of others. Although other views are included in this book as well, my main focus is on my own conclusions.

Deductive Framework

One of the problems we face with regard to any doctrine is having a theological framework within which to develop our thoughts. In other words, we need a systematic theology of the Spirit. Sometimes we interpret isolated verses without any relationship to the entire subject that we are discussing. We need to see any given experience, such as the baptism in the Spirit, in the light of all that the Bible says about the Holy Spirit. Only then will we have a balanced and complete experience of the Spirit.

Based on all of my inductive studies, I have written this book as a systematic theology about the Holy Spirit and our relationship with Him. It is a deductive approach to the teachings of the Word about the Spirit. The emphasis is on the Word as it applies to our lives. Without this application, we just have a lot of information that is not too relevant for us. With the application, our lives are dramatically changed.

Unity and Diversity

Through our inductive study, we have observed both unity and diversity among the authors of the books of the Bible on the subject of the Holy Spirit. In recent times, there has been a considerable amount of study by scholars with regard to Luke and Paul. Both similarities and differences between them are noted. This is all good, but more time should be devoted to the Old Testament, to John, and to the other New Testament authors. Even though there is both unity and diversity, all of the authors are complementary to each other.

In this book, I have included some summary comments concerning the Old Testament and the transition between the Old Testament and the New Testament. The opening chapter is devoted to the theme of Christ being the central figure in the transition. As far as the New Testament is concerned, I have focused on Luke, John, and Paul. This focus appears in several chapters. Any comparison involves similarities and differences. These points of comparison are apparent from our inductive studies.

Ten Topics

As I studied the work of the Spirit, I did not begin with a complete set of predetermined issues to investigate. Indeed, I have derived issues from the biblical authors themselves, followed the texts throughout the Bible, and have reported what I discovered. At the same time, some issues arose out of current theological interests.

Our approach in this book is to deal with the issues in a topical way. The ten chapters deal with topics that present a broad outline of our relationship with the Holy Spirit. At the end of each chapter, I have written a conclusion. Drawing from these conclusions, I am presenting the following preview of the content in this book.

1. *Christ is Central*. At the outset, it is important to know that Christ is the central figure in the redemption story. Without Him, we as human beings are lost and without eternal hope. Our situation is desperate. So we must turn to Him in faith. Through faith in Christ, we have hope. We know, of course, that the Father, the Son, and the Holy Spirit all have specific roles in our salvation. Sometimes their roles overlap. Moreover, whenever one Person of the Godhead is involved, all three Persons are involved. Nevertheless, by God's design, Jesus Christ is the central figure.

2. *The Powerful Persuader*. The Holy Spirit is a powerful persuader. We know that the Holy Spirit has persuasively drawn us to Jesus. Because He has persuaded us that Christ is our Savior, our hearts are full of gratitude to God for His saving grace. The Spirit has illuminated our minds with the Word of God and has drawn us

inwardly to the One who can redeem us from our sins. We stand in awe at the atoning work of Christ our Lord.

Moreover, we are full of faith because we know that, when we witness, the Holy Spirit is at work in His wonderful way to persuade men and women to come to Jesus in faith. We are not alone in our efforts to fulfill the Great Commission. We are working with God Himself. Our God is seeking out the lost and is welcoming them to come to Jesus. He will help us find all those who will respond in faith to Christ. This gives us great hope that our mission, under God, will be accomplished.

3. *Becoming Sons of God.* Just as Paul does in Galatians 3:26, in this book, the term "sons of God" is used generically, referring to both male and female offsprings. In this chapter, we have focused on how we become sons of God. We can rejoice in the fact that, through faith in Christ, we have the position of a son of God. Throughout our lives, we have the joy of an experiential relationship with God. We interact with the Father, Son, and Holy Spirit as sons and servants of our Lord. When we believe in Christ, we receive the double gift of union with Christ and reception of the Spirit. This double gift is bestowed in an objective sense. As we live with Christ, our experience of Christ and the Spirit develops. All of this gives us a growing sense of assurance that we are sons of God.

4. *Giving and Receiving the Spirit.* An inductive study of terms that the Bible uses about the giving and receiving of the Holy Spirit reveals considerable flexibility. The terms are amazingly flexible, varied, and rich in imagery. Expositors sometimes define these terms too narrowly and limit their meaning. When we do this, our understanding of many passages is impoverished. Many theological arguments could be resolved simply by applying more inclusive interpretations of the crucial terms.

As an example, some scholars hold that, when a person believes in Christ, he "receives" the Spirit and that this is a one-time moment only. They may emphasize the union of our spirit with the Spirit of God or the subjective experiential nature of receiving the Spirit. Other scholars view the term more flexibly. When it is, we can see that believers have received the Spirit, are receiving the Spirit, and will receive the Spirit.

5. *Types of Experience.* As we study, the picture we get is that our Christian life begins with the objective, non-experiential acts of God. Immediately, we begin to experience the works of God within and through our lives. The experiences we have may be quiet and almost unobserved, or crisis moments of great intensity, or the continuous presence of the Spirit, the experience of the Spirit in various measures, and His presence in many dimensions of the Spirit's life and work. With all of this experience available to us, we can truly count ourselves as beloved sons of God.

6. *Dimensions of the Spirit.* Our relationship with the Spirit has many dimensions. Through a study of all of the authors in the Bible, we can recognize a great variety of dimensions that affect our lives. These dimensions are to some extent overlapping, affecting all aspects of our lives. We have no aspect of our lives untouched. Instead, the Spirit has an impact on every detail of our existence. Truly, we are friends, sons, and servants of the great God of the universe. What a privilege is ours! We must keep ourselves open to the realization of all that God grants to us.

7. *Eternal Life and Truth.* In this chapter, my emphasis is on the dimensions of eternal life and truth. The Father, Son, and Holy Spirit all have a part in giving us eternal life. Through faith in Christ and through the work of the Spirit, we can have eternal life. In addition, we can enjoy the fellowship of the saints who are growing in their knowledge of truth and in the image of Christ. Concerning truth, both Christ and the Spirit are said to be the truth. Moreover, the truth is what Christ taught and what the Holy Spirit brings to our remembrance. What the entire Word of God teaches is truth. As we learn and know the truth, we should live the truth. In other words, truth is truth applied and lived by us.

8. *The Baptism in the Spirit.* A subject of great interest to all believers is the baptism in the Spirit. In this chapter, I present various viewpoints about baptism in the Spirit, give the Scriptural data concerning this aspect of our spiritual lives, present the relevance of the baptism metaphor for baptism in the Spirit, discuss the baptism in the Spirit at Pentecost, and deal with special issues. For example, some scholars narrowly define the metaphor, but others believe it can be used with different meanings.

Many expositors hold that baptism in the Spirit has to do with the entry of believers into the body of Christ. The contrasting view is that baptism in the Spirit is an experience subsequent to the initiation of Christian life. Proponents of this view may differ as to the exact purpose of this experience. The proposed purposes include assurance of salvation, purity of life, and empowerment for witness. Some scholars believe that the phrase "baptism in the Spirit" can refer to both entry into the body of Christ and empowerment for service.

9. *Fruit and Gifts.* As believers in Christ, we have the privilege of a very close relationship with the Triune God. God dwells in us, and we dwell in Him. The Spirit of God exalts Christ and applies His redemptive work to us. He helps us grow and develop the fruit of the Spirit so that we are like Christ in our attitudes and relationships with others. In addition, the Spirit gives us gifts that enable us to minister out of love in an effective manner to the body of Christ. Let us manifest both the gifts and the fruit of the Spirit.

10. *Taking "Not Yet" Seriously.* Our journey with Christ began when we accepted Christ through faith. It has continued ever since. When we abide in Christ, all of the experiences of life contribute to our development. Even times of adversity have their positive impact in the long run. Then, there are many moments of open and positive blessing that give us great spiritual enjoyment.

Our lives are devoted not only to reaching full stature but also to reaching, teaching, and training others. They, in turn, will grow in the image of Christ and help to train a growing body of believers who will be engaged in the work of the kingdom of God. Our relationship with the Holy Spirit is an essential part of making our spiritual journey the very best that it can be. We are becoming what we are.

Resources

This book is a systematic theology about our relationship with the Holy Spirit. The content is drawn from the three volumes I wrote entitled *A Biblical Theology of the Holy Spirit.* I included many footnotes in those three volumes, but I have not included any of them in this book. For sources, please refer to those three volumes.

At the end of this book, I have included a Scripture index, as well as an index of transliterated Greek terms and a comprehensive bibliography on the Holy Spirit. The comprehensive bibliography on the Holy Spirit is taken from the three volume work and is an excellent resource for those who want to study further.

My Hope

My hope is that all believers who want to give serious study to their relationship with the Holy Spirit will find these studies useful and inspiring. Also, it is my desire that busy pastors and teachers in local churches will find a wealth of information in this study that will be helpful as they prepare their own studies on the subject of the Holy Spirit. Some may even want to teach these chapters somewhat as they are. Either way, I would be very much rewarded for making the study.

Having made the study, it is abundantly clear how Christ-centered the biblical authors were in their thinking. It is equally clear that every aspect of a Christian's life should be affected by the presence and leading of the Spirit. My prayer is that, as believers, we all regularly and powerfully experience the divine presence and power of the Holy Spirit of God.

ACKNOWLEDGEMENTS

It is my privilege to acknowledge the inestimable value of the contributions made by others to this theological project. I cannot say enough to thank Dr. Jim Richardson for his work as the editor of this volume. Given his background in biblical languages and in seminary teaching, he was the ideal editor. Dr. Richardson has done outstanding work in improving the presentation of all the content. Also, I was honored to have Dr. Anthony Palma read the manuscript. One of his main interests has been the study of the Holy Spirit. His work in this field of study and his knowledge of Greek were helpful to me.

Because this volume is based on the three volumes that I wrote entitled *A Biblical Theology of the Holy Spirit*, I will repeat here the acknowledgements from that work. In the General Introduction, I wrote these comments.

It has been my joy over many years to study the Scriptures in the Bible concerning the Holy Spirit. I published some of the material in these volumes on the Internet, but I had not completed the task, and I had not published the material in print. It was Dr. Carl Chrisner, the Dean of the Graduate School of Theology at Global University who envisioned the completion of the project. He urged me to put everything in print in textbook form. Given his interest, I agreed to finish the task. At the same time, he assigned Dr. Jim Richardson to be the General Editor of all the material.

Also, I deeply appreciate all those scholars with whom I have interacted over the years. It was my privilege to discuss various interpretations with many leading biblical scholars concerning their views. A special word of gratitude goes to the Greek and Hebrew scholars who have read my manuscripts. These scholars include Dr. French Arrington, Dr. Roger Cotton, Dr. Ben Aker, and Jackie Braswell. Given their expertise in Greek and/or Hebrew, it is helpful to know that they especially have reviewed our interpretations involving the biblical languages. Although their own views may vary in some cases from mine, I am grateful for the time they devoted to reviewing our manuscripts.

Finally, I owe a debt of thanks to my wife and our two sons. Much of my early research was done before our sons left home to go to college. They were supportive then, and still are, of my interest in the study of the Holy Spirit. George is a pastor, and Mark is a missionary. I pray that these studies will be a blessing to them, as well as many others, in their ministries. Above all, I owe much to Esther, my beloved wife. Along with being fully involved in our life-long missionary ministry, she patiently listened and supported my efforts with regard to this study. She has "made all the difference" in the initiation and completion of this work.

—George M. Flattery, Ed.D.

January 15, 2012

ACRONYMS AND ABBREVIATIONS

AG	Assemblies of God
AGWM	Assemblies of God World Missions
ARV	American Revised Version (see ASV)
ASV	American Standard Version
AV	Authorized Version (see KJV)
BDAG	Bauer, Danker, Arndt, and Gingrich
BDB	Brown, Driver, and Briggs
ERV	English Revised Version
KJV	King James Version
LXX	Septuagint
NAB	New American Bible
NASB	New American Standard Bible
NASB[95]	New American Standard Bible, 1995 update
NEB	New English Bible
NIV	New International Version
NLT	New Living Translation
NRSV	New Revised Standard Version
RSV	Revised Standard Version
TLB	The Living Bible
TDNT	Kittel's *Theological Dictionary of the New Testament*

CHAPTER ONE
CHRIST IS CENTRAL

As believers in Christ, we serve the Triune God. The Father, the Son, and the Holy Spirit are one eternal God. God has no beginning and will have no end. Amazingly, our eternal and infinite God desires to have fellowship with us. Our fellowship with Him is possible because He has provided a way of salvation for us. All three Persons of the Godhead are involved in His saving activity, but each Person has special roles.

Our discussions in this series are devoted to a study of the Holy Spirit. Our focus will be on the role of the Spirit in the salvation story. In this story, the redemptive work of Christ is central. So our doctrine of the Spirit's role in salvation is Christ-centered. The Holy Spirit communicates about Christ, applies His redemptive work to our lives, inspires our worship, and empowers us in our ministries.

In this chapter, we will compare the role of the Holy Spirit as presented in the Old and the New Testaments, discuss the transition that took place through the redemptive work of Christ, discuss the events of resurrection day, and present Jesus as the exalted Lord and Christ. This exalted Lord bestows the abiding Spirit upon us. The presence of the Spirit assures us of our salvation.

Testaments Compared

When we compare the role of the Spirit in the Old and New Testaments, we should consider both similarities and differences. There is great similarity and continuity between the work of the Spirit in the Old Testament and in the New Testament. However, there are several differences as well that give us an enriched New Testament experience.

1. *Promise and Fulfillment.* The Old Testament promises include the coming of the Spirit upon the Messiah who will be the redeemer of the people. The relevant passages include Psalm 2:2, 7; 1 Samuel 2:10; Isaiah 11:2; 42:1, 61:1–2; and Zechariah 12:10. In the New Testament, we see the realization of these promises. For example, at the baptism of

Jesus (Luke 3:22), a voice out of heaven says, "Thou art my beloved Son, in Thee I am well-pleased." This passage is a fulfillment of Psalm 2:7 and Isaiah 42:1. The fulfilled promises include the death, burial, and resurrection of Christ. The redemptive work of Christ is central to the transition from the Old to the New Testament.

2. *Redemptive Work.* Old Testament saints were saved in anticipation of the redemptive work of Christ. The Holy Spirit had His great influence on them, but something greater was coming. Now, because Christ has accomplished His redemptive work, the Holy Spirit can apply it to our lives. Jesus came to earth to dwell among us. He died for our sins, was buried, and rose again. The Spirit was at work throughout this process. The Holy Spirit was present among the Old Testament saints, but His presence is far greater now.

3. *Givers of the Spirit.* In both the Old and New Testament, God gives the Spirit. We can use the term "gives" broadly to include such terms as "pour out" and "come upon." In the New Testament, Jesus also is regarded as a giver of the Spirit (John 15:26). He sends the Spirit to work among us, in us, and through us. Moreover, Jesus is the baptizer in the Holy Spirit (John 1:33; Luke 3:16).

4. *The Spirit and the Saints.* To some degree, the Holy Spirit was present in the daily lives of the Old Testament saints (Ps. 51:10–12). In addition, chosen people were empowered for service. In the New Testament, all who believe in Christ are indwelt by the Spirit and enjoy His abiding presence. Also, all people can be empowered to serve. The Holy Spirit is poured out upon all flesh (Acts 2:17–18). Thus, there is a democratization of the Spirit's empowerment.

5. *Covenants.* All that the Spirit did under the old covenant, including empowerment for service, is brought forward and included under the new covenant. Paul connects the Spirit with the new covenant. Paul regards himself, and others, as "servants of a new covenant, not of the letter, but of the Spirit" (2 Cor. 3:6). New covenant ministry is "the ministry of the Spirit" (2 Cor. 3:8).

The crux of the new covenant is a new heart. Ezekiel 36:26–27 states that the God will give us new hearts and put His Spirit within us. Under the new covenant, as Jeremiah 31:31–33 indicates, the laws of God will be written in the hearts of men. These passages are being fulfilled as Paul ministers. He writes that the Corinthians "are a letter of Christ, cared for by us, written not with ink, but the Spirit of the living God, not on tablets of stone, but on tablets of human hearts" (2 Cor. 3:3).

The Transition

As our comparison of the Testaments asserts, a transition in the role of the Spirit occurred because of the incarnation and life of Christ on earth. The four Gospels record the activities of Christ during this time of transition. The transition has to do with the incarnation, ministry, death, and resurrection of Christ.

1. *The Spirit upon Jesus.* There is a close relationship between Jesus and the Holy Spirit. Jesus was conceived (Matt. 1:20) of the Holy Spirit. Another crisis moment came right after Jesus was baptized by John the Baptist. According to Luke 3:22, "the Holy Spirit descended upon Him [Jesus] in bodily form like a dove." John 1:32 adds "and He remained upon Him." Jesus was endowed with an abiding presence of the Spirit.

Luke does not say that a dove descended. Rather, the Holy Spirit descended in "bodily form like a dove." Like most metaphors, the term "dove" is very flexible. A dove can be representative of such characteristics as peace, friendliness, purity, meekness, graciousness, and others. It is best not to limit the meaning of the term.

2. *Jesus Ministered in the Spirit.* After the temptation of Jesus, He left the Jordan and "was led about by the Spirit in the wilderness" (Luke 4:1). Then, He returned to Galilee "in the power of the Spirit" (Luke 4:14). The news about Him quickly spread throughout the surrounding district. The manifested power of the Spirit attracts a crowd.

When Jesus was at the synagogue in Nazareth, He read Isaiah 61:1–2 as He spoke to the gathered audience (Luke 4:18–19). Jesus claimed that He was anointed to preach the Gospel to the poor, to proclaim release to the captives, to bring recovery of sight to the blind, and to set free those who are downtrodden. In addition, Luke records this declaration by Peter, "*You know of* Jesus of Nazareth, how God anointed Him with the Holy Spirit and with power, and *how* He went about doing good and healing all who were oppressed by the devil, for God was with Him" (Acts 10:38).

3. *Jesus Must Be Glorified.* The Holy Spirit would apply the redemptive work of Christ to all believers. The full work of the Spirit, however, could not take place until Jesus was glorified. The glorification of Jesus specifically includes His death (John 12:23–24) and resurrection (Acts 3:13–15). In John 7:37–39, John sets forth the truth that the disciples would receive the Spirit when Jesus would be glorified. He writes:

> [37]Now on the last day, the great *day* of the feast, Jesus stood and cried out, saying, "If anyone is thirsty, let him come to Me and drink. [38]He who believes in Me, as the Scripture said, 'From his innermost being will flow rivers of living water.'" [39]But this He spoke of the Spirit, whom those who believed in Him were to receive; for the Spirit was not yet *given*, because Jesus was not yet glorified.

The word "given" is not in the Greek text, but most commentators agree that John was not intending to say that the Spirit did not exist before the glorification of Jesus. It surely means that He could not yet apply the redemptive work of Christ because it had not yet been accomplished.

4. *Jesus and the Helper.* In John 14:16–17, Jesus speaks about the transition that would occur with regard to Him and the Holy Spirit. The main point is that Jesus was going away, but the Helper would be with (*meta*) them forever. Jesus makes this announcement.

> [16]"I will ask the Father, and He will give you another Helper, that He may be with [*meta*] you forever; [17]*that is* the Spirit of truth, whom the world cannot receive, because it does not see Him or know Him, *but* you know Him because He abides [*menei*] with [*para*] you and will be [*estai*] in [*en*] you.

Some writers hold that the Greek prepositions in this passage explain the difference in the Spirit's work before and after Christ's glorification. According to them, the Spirit was with (*para*), by the side of the disciples before the glorification, but afterwards the Spirit will be in (*en*) them. It may be that the preposition *en* suggests a new inwardness to the work of the Spirit. However, not too much should be deduced from the prepositions. They are subject to various meanings and interpretations.

Several points will illustrate this flexibility. The statements that "you know Him" and "He abides with (*para*) you" apply not only to the disciples who were with Jesus but also to all disciples now. Now, the Father and the Son will make their abode with (*para*) believers. This would suggest that the Holy Spirit does, too. The prepositions *meta* (v. 16) and *en* (v. 17) both apply now.

5. *Jesus Baptizes in the Spirit*. When John the Baptist baptized Jesus, he declared that Jesus "will baptize [*baptisei*] people in the Holy Spirit (Matt. 3:11; Mark 1:8; Luke 3:16). Using the future tense, these authors speak of a future baptism. However, John uses the present participle in John 1:33. According to his report, the Baptist said, "I did not recognize Him, but He who sent me to baptize in water said to me, 'He upon whom you see the Spirit descending and remaining upon Him, this is the One who baptizes [*baptizōn*] in the Holy Spirit.'" The present participle can represent a rhetorical future, but clearly its primary reference is to something currently happening.

When Jesus was near the end of His earthly ministry, He dealt with the concerns of the disciples about His going away. He comforted them with this declaration: "When the Helper comes, whom I will send to you from the Father, *that is* the Spirit of truth who proceeds from the Father, He will testify about Me" (John 15:26). As John 14:16 indicates, the Father, too, is a giver of the Spirit.

Resurrection Day

Resurrection day was a dramatic day in the history of the world. The death, burial, and resurrection of Christ changed the world. As I understand the events of the day, Jesus ascended to the Father on the morning of the resurrection and later, in the evening, bestowed the Holy Spirit. We turn now to a short discussion of these events.

1. *Ascension*. As John reports the story, Mary Magdalene (John 20:1) came to the tomb of Jesus and found it empty. After Mary ran to tell Peter, she returned to the tomb, stood outside, and wept. It was then that she beheld Jesus standing by. After a short exchange, Jesus

said to her (John 20:17), "Stop clinging to Me, for I have not yet ascended to the Father; but go to My brethren and say to them, 'I ascend [*anabainō*] to My Father and your Father, and My God and your God.'" Jesus, using the present tense, says "I am ascending to My Father." Although this can be read as a rhetorical future, I believe He ascended right away.

The sequence of events in Luke and Acts is different than in John, but the two reports are harmonious. Luke describes the public ascension of Jesus in Acts 1:9. This can be harmonized with John 20:17 by either translating John 20:17 as "I am about to ascend" or "I am ascending." As expressed above, my view is that the first ascension of Jesus was on resurrection morning. His public ascension came later. Either interpretation is possible. Jesus already was resurrected, and His glorified body was not limited as to time and space.

2. *Jesus Bestowed the Spirit.* A great scene occurred on the evening of Resurrection day. In my view, John 20:19–23 and Luke 24:36–49 belong to the same evening event. Jesus appeared to His disciples as they were shut in behind closed doors and talked with the disciples. Then, as John reports in verse 22, Jesus "breathed on them and said to them, 'Receive the Holy Spirit.'" Although some scholars regard this as symbolic, it seems best to me to accept this as an actual bestowal of the Spirit. Before His death, Jesus taught about the coming Helper. It is natural to assume that He was bestowing the Helper to them. All that the promised Helper would do is now possible.

Jesus commented further about the Spirit. In Luke 24:49, Jesus says, "And behold, I am sending forth [*apostellō*] the promise of My Father upon you; but you are to stay in the city until you are clothed with power from on high." Jesus used the present tense. The disciples received a measure of the Spirit's power that evening, but they were to wait in Jerusalem until they were fully empowered. The full outpouring of the Spirit would come on the Day of Pentecost.

The Exalted Jesus

Now, we will examine Luke's report in Acts 2:31–36. In this passage, Peter tells us that God raised up Jesus and exalted Him to the Father's right hand. Peter declares that Jesus received and poured out the Spirit. Furthermore, God made Jesus both Lord and Christ.

1. *God Raised Up Jesus.* Acts 2:31–32 makes two points abundantly clear: (1) God raised up Jesus from the dead, and (2) the disciples were witnesses concerning the resurrection. In this passage, Peter cites David as saying, "he looked ahead and spoke of the resurrection of the Christ, that HE WAS NEITHER ABANDONED TO HADES, NOR DID His flesh SUFFER DECAY" (v. 31). Then, in verse 32, Peter says, "This Jesus God raised up again, to which we are all witnesses."

First, it is important to notice that it was God who raised up Jesus. This is the repeated testimony of the Scriptures. The resurrection of Christ was no magician's trick. It was not an accident in the normal course of nature. It was, instead, a definite act of God and a demonstration of His power. Nothing less than an act of God would be convincing to the Jews. In addition, the Holy Spirit had a role in the resurrection and exaltation of Jesus. The writer of Hebrews says that Christ offered Himself without blemish to God "through the eternal Spirit" (9:14).

Our text demonstrates that Jesus was the Son of God—both divine and human. This point had to be established. The people in Jerusalem had seen him tried, beaten, suffering on the cross, and dying. They saw him bleeding as he hung between two thieves. They saw the soldiers take him down and knew that he was buried in the tomb. As far as they were concerned, the rolling of the stone in front of his grave settled the matter. He was just a man whose life was over. But the evidence put forward in our text demonstrates who Jesus really is.

Second, Peter declares that "we are witnesses" to the fact that God raised up Jesus. Peter was among those who were eye-witnesses. When Peter arrived at the tomb on resurrection morning, the tomb was empty (Luke 24:12). He was one of the disciples (Luke 24:34) to whom Jesus appeared after His resurrection. Other witnesses, including us, are those who testify to what they come to know in some way. As witnesses, we are to tell people everywhere that God raised up Jesus.

2. *Jesus Was Exalted.* Peter speaks of Christ as "having been exalted" and "having received" the promise of the Holy Spirit. He uses two aorist participles to tell us what had happened at some time before Jesus poured forth the Spirit. The exaltation of Christ preceded the outpouring of the Spirit, and it further defines who Jesus is. Our knowledge about Christ and, henceforth, our witness deepen! In Acts 2:33–35, Peter declares:

> [33]Therefore having been exalted [*hupsōtheis*] to the right hand of God, and having received [*labōn*] from the Father the promise of the Holy Spirit, He has poured forth this which you both see and hear. [34]For it was not David who ascended into heaven, but he himself says: "THE LORD SAID TO MY LORD, 'SIT AT MY RIGHT HAND [35]UNTIL I MAKE YOUR ENEMIES A FOOTSTOOL FOR YOUR FEET.'"

There are several elements to exaltation. As we examine the New Testament usage of this word, a beautiful and meaningful picture emerges. We come to a greater understanding of the stature, character, and power of Jesus Christ.

First, Jesus was exalted through death. Jesus spoke in John 3:14; 8:28; and 12:32–34 of His being lifted up. He was referring to His exaltation through his death and crucifixion. In all these passages, John uses the same Greek word (*hupsoō*) that Luke uses in Acts 2:33. He would be lifted up, or exalted, upon the cross. Certainly, Jesus was "lifted up" or "exalted" physically at the cross. Beyond this, we might readily view this as the first step toward being exalted in the ascension and resurrection. Unless you approach this with great spiritual understanding, it is hard to grasp. Jesus was crucified on the way to, and even as a part of, being exalted in honor!

Second, as Peter uses the word, the exaltation of Christ has to do with the ascension (Acts 2:32–33; 5:30–31). We already have discussed the resurrection. Now we will speak about the ascension. Peter declares in Acts 2:33 and 5:31 that Jesus was exalted to the right hand of the Father. In order to be at the right hand of the Father, Jesus had to ascend into heaven. Thus, the exaltation includes the ascension.

Third, the exaltation of Jesus placed Him at the right hand of the Father. In Acts 2:34, Peter cites Psalm 110:1 which says: "The Lord says to my Lord: 'Sit at My right hand, until I make Thine enemies a footstool for Thy feet.'" Peter declares that it was not David who ascended into heaven, but it was Christ who ascended to sit at the right hand of the Father. In this way, Jesus was exalted.

Fourth, God's right hand is a place of authority, power, and utmost honor. The "right hand" of God is spoken about frequently in the New Testament. For example, Psalm 110:1 is cited in all three of the Synoptic Gospels (Matt. 22:44; Mark 12:36; and Luke 20:42–43). It was also cited in Hebrews 1:13. The fulfillment of Psalm 110:1 is a major point of emphasis in the New Testament.

The apostle Paul prayed for the Ephesians (1:18–23) that they would be spiritually enlightened with regard to Christ. In his prayer, he states that God raised Jesus from the dead and seated him at His right hand. Through this action, God bestowed great power upon Christ. God subjected all things to Jesus and made Him "head over all things to the church, which is His body."

Yes, Jesus is at the right hand of the Father. What does this mean for us and for the future? The Scriptures are abundantly clear. Consider some of the passages which deal with the impact of Jesus being at the right hand of the Father.

- This Jesus, who sits at the right hand of the Father, is "the Son of God" (Luke 22:69–70). Only He could qualify to sit in the seat of power over the universe.

- This Jesus, who sits at the right hand of the Father, is our High Priest. He offered "one sacrifice for sins for all time" (Heb. 10:12). He died for you and for me that we might have eternal life. He will protect His investment of His life in us!

- This Jesus, who sits at the right hand of the Father, is the "author and perfecter" of faith (Heb. 12:2). The lifted up Christ draws us to Him, and He leads us in our faith to perfection.

- This Jesus, who sits at the right hand of the Father, "intercedes" (Rom. 8:34) for us. Pause a moment and think about it! The Lord of all the universe prays for us.

- This Jesus, who sits at the right hand of the Father, worked with His disciples and confirmed the Word with signs following (Mark 16:19–20). Today, He is with us as we do His work. He is right beside us as we witness.

- This Jesus, who sits at the right hand of the Father, conquered His enemies through His death and resurrection. The enemies of Christ will be made a footstool for His feet (Heb. 10:13).

- This Jesus, who sits at the right hand of the Father, will return. We will see Him "coming on the clouds of heaven" (Matt. 26:64).

3. *Jesus Received and Poured Out the Spirit.* Peter now turns his attention to Christ and the Holy Spirit (Acts 2:33). This verse, too, will further support who Jesus is. The very claim that Jesus poured out the Spirit will demonstrate that He is Himself God. No one but God could pour out the Spirit of God. In verse 33, Peter states: "And having received from the Father the promise of the Holy Spirit, He has poured forth this which you both see and hear."

First, we have another term describing what happened to Jesus. The first term was "having been exalted." Now, we have "having received" the promise of the Holy Spirit. Before pouring out the Spirit, Jesus received the Spirit.

As we have noted, this is not the first experience of Christ with the Spirit. The Spirit had a part in the incarnation of Christ (Matt. 1:20). The Spirit of God came upon Mary, the mother of Jesus (Luke 1:35). The Spirit "descended upon" Jesus at His baptism (Luke 3:22). Jesus ministered throughout His ministry in the power of the Spirit (Acts 10:38). As I understand Romans 1:4, the Spirit had a role in raising Jesus from the dead. None of this precluded His reception of the Spirit at His exaltation.

Second, Peter uses the phrase "promise of the Holy Spirit." The coming of the Spirit had long been promised. Jesus now received the promised Spirit so that He could pour out the Spirit. When Luke refers to the promise of the Spirit, he has in mind primarily the empowering presence of the Spirit. The Spirit empowers us to witness. As Paul uses the term, the entire presence and work of the

Spirit is included. He uses the term comprehensively, including the power to be a witness.

Third, we turn to the outpouring of the Spirit upon the disciples. The Spirit "poured forth" resulted in an experience that could be seen and heard. It was "this which you both see and hear." The Spirit filled the disciples (Acts 2:4) who then spoke in other tongues. The people heard them "speaking of the mighty deeds of God" (Acts 2:11). What the crowd saw and heard was the Spirit empowering the disciples to speak prophetically and to witness.

4. *God Made Jesus both Lord and Christ*. Peter has been building toward His climactic point. He exhorts, "Therefore let all the house of Israel know for certain that God has made Him both Lord and Christ—this Jesus whom you crucified" (Acts 2:36). God raised up Jesus. God exalted Him to the right hand of the Father, and gave Him all authority, power, and honor. Jesus received the promised Spirit. Then, Jesus poured out the Spirit upon the disciples. The conclusion was now inescapable. This Jesus was the Son of God. God had made Him both Lord and Christ!

First, Peter is ready to proclaim that this Jesus whom they crucified was Lord. That Jesus is Lord is absolutely essential to our witness and to our lives as Christians. The apostle Paul, in Philippians 2:5–11, exalts the Lordship of Christ. He puts the story together succinctly and in the most beautiful of terms.

Second, Jesus is Christ. Our word "Christ" is from the Greek word *Christos* which means "anointed One." The title "Messiah" is a translation from Hebrew, and it also means "anointed One." Christ is the anointed One and awaited Messiah. There is only one Messiah, the anointed One, and He poured out the anointing upon the disciples. This truth is equally essential to our witness. Jesus is both Lord and Christ.

Third, through the redemptive work of Christ, a new relationship between Christ and the Spirit was established. Later, Luke calls the Spirit the "Spirit of Jesus" (Acts 16:7). The Spirit is poured forth by Jesus. The Spirit and Jesus are one, yet they are different. This is a part of the mystery of the divine Trinity.

5. *The Gift of the Spirit.* The comment that God made Jesus to be both Lord and Christ was Peter's closing remark in his sermon on the Day of Pentecost. After making this assertion, Peter issued an invitation to the audience. In Acts 2:38–39, we read:

> [38]Peter *said* to them, "Repent, and each of you be baptized in the name of Jesus Christ for the forgiveness of your sins; and you will receive the gift of the Holy Spirit. [39]For the promise is for you and your children and for all who are far off, as many as the Lord our God will call to Himself."

As we interpret these verses, let us keep in mind what Peter spoke on the Day of Pentecost. What did he mean by "receive" the gift of the Holy Spirit? He had just cited Joel 2:28–32. Peter knew what the Old Testament promised about the Spirit, and He knew what Jesus had taught. At the time, the epistles of Paul had not been written. We cannot limit the meaning of the term, but it seems reasonable that the main thing he had in mind was the baptism in the Spirit that the disciples had just experienced.

Conclusion

The Father, the Son, and the Holy Spirit all have specific roles in salvation. Sometimes their roles overlap. Whenever one Person of the Godhead is involved, all three Persons are involved.

Nevertheless, Jesus Christ is the central figure in the salvation story. Without Him, we as human beings are lost and without eternal hope. Our situation is desperate. So we must turn to Him in faith. Through faith in Christ, we have hope. When we come to faith, we are united with Christ and indwelt by the Spirit. The redemptive work of Christ is applied to us by the Holy Spirit. Moreover, the Holy Spirit empowers us for witness and service.

CHAPTER TWO

THE POWERFUL PERSUADER

The Gospel commands us to be witnesses at home and abroad, nearby and far away. We know this, but we are sometimes stymied by a problem. We want to win people to Christ, but we seem to be unable to speak persuasively to them. At times, we may feel inadequate, if not helpless.

Our problem is made worse because the world is filled with many religions and worldviews. Because of the vast increase in communications and the movement of people, many people are seeking to make their views known throughout the world. The battle for the minds of men is raging as never before. Even so, we must enter the arena and persuasively present Christ.

Many times, we wonder how and why people will respond to Christ. In some cases, especially when we have done a lot to reach them, we question why they reject Him. In other cases, we are joyously surprised when people come to faith. It may be that we have not done much to reach them, but they turn to Christ.

We must realize that ultimately it is our Triune God who persuades men to believe in Christ. The Father, the Son, and the Holy Spirit all have distinct roles. In addition, the Word of God is an effective instrument in God's hands. Other means that God uses include circumstances, our environment, our friends and enemies, and the difficulties encountered in life. God is not limited.

Most believers remember how God worked in their own lives to draw them to Christ. They remember how God found them, the circumstances that they were in at the time, the loving pull of the Spirit to believe in Jesus, and the change that ensued as a result of their response. In short, they remember their conversion experience. These memories are helpful as they witness to others. There is great power in their own testimonies.

My purpose in this lesson is to present the Holy Spirit in His role as the Powerful Persuader. We will consider the issue of free will and predestination, the Spirit's empowerment of Jesus and the believers, the Spirit's persuasive inner voice, and the Spirit at work convincing the world of sin, righteousness, and judgment. As we study these truths, we will be encouraged to speak boldly for Christ.

Free Will and Predestination

The subject of how and why people are persuaded to follow Christ raises the issue of free will and predestination. Throughout the history of the church, this has been a huge subject of theological discussion. The Bible has a great deal to say about both free will and the sovereignty of God. Although we sometimes have difficulty reconciling these truths, we know that there is no contradiction in the mind of God. As background for our study of the work of the Spirit in persuasion, we will make a few comments on the issue.

1. *Teaching of Jesus.* Jesus brings this issue into focus in His Bread of Life discourse (John 6:37, 39–40, 44–45, 65). In John 6:37, Jesus stresses the Father's action, our human responsibility, and His own response. The Father gives people to the Son, the people respond by coming to Jesus, and Jesus readily accepts them. Those who come to Jesus do so by believing in Him (John 6:39–40). When they believe, they come to the Father as well as to Jesus. Later, Jesus says that no one comes to the Father except through Jesus (John 14:6).

The Father both "gives" and "draws" people to Jesus. No one can come to Jesus unless the Father "draws" (*helkusēi*) him to Jesus (John 6:44). Unless this has been granted (John 6:65) by the Father, no one can come. Using the same Greek verb, Jesus declares that He, as well as the Father, "draws" (*helkusō*) men to Himself (John 12:32). Because of His death on the cross, men are drawn to Him. Jesus was "lifted up" or "exalted" by His death. The manner of His death communicates His great love, His identification with us, and His willingness to suffer that we might live. This great act of Jesus, as well as His words, challenges men to believe in Him.

2. *Questions.* As we consider these matters, questions arise. We might ask, "Does the Father select some to be saved and then give them to Jesus?" Or, "Does the Father choose to give those who

already have responded in faith?" "Which comes first, the giving or the believing?" It is not my purpose here to fully discuss these questions. I would just say that my own view is that the Father actively seeks the salvation of all men. He gives those to Jesus who respond in faith to Him. Those who respond in faith receive the Father's approval. Our human responsibility is to respond in faith to all that God does to draw us to Christ. Also, we remain totally grateful for the grace of God and His initiative.

As we think about these questions, we must realize that the Bible teaches both moral responsibility and the sovereignty of God. Even though we will not fully reconcile these truths, we should accept them as complementary rather than contradictory. The fact that God is in control is a great comfort to us all. At the same time, we know we are responsible for our actions.

3. *Purpose.* My purpose in this chapter is to discuss the role of the Holy Spirit in persuading men to believe in Christ. No matter how one reconciles free will and predestination, the role of the Holy Spirit is clearly presented in the Scriptures. So we will turn our attention to this subject.

The Spirit's Empowerment

As we study the work of the Spirit, we discover that He is a very powerful persuader. Because the Holy Spirit is at work, our efforts in building the kingdom of God bear fruit. Without Him, our efforts would not be productive. The Word of God is a persuasive tool in the hands of the Spirit. The Spirit persuasively draws people to Christ. Several passages of Scripture bear this out.

1. *The Spirit Empowers Jesus.* Jesus was anointed to preach the Gospel to the poor, to proclaim release to the captives, to proclaim recovery of sight to the blind, and to set free those who are downtrodden (Luke 4:16–21). Through His anointed ministry, people were attracted to Him (Luke 4:22). All aspects of life would be enhanced through faith in Him. The central focus of His mission was to draw men to Himself as Savior, but through faith in Christ, the believers would experience comprehensive results.

The Holy Spirit anointed Jesus to fulfill His mission. In Acts 10:38, Luke writes, "*You know of* Jesus of Nazareth, how God anointed Him with the Holy Spirit and with power, and *how* He went about doing good and healing all who were oppressed by the devil, for God was with Him." The divine-human Son of God ministered in the power of the Spirit. As the Son of God, Jesus had divine power, but He normally operated in the power of the Spirit. This was His voluntary choice. This is why we speak of the "self-emptying" of Christ (Phil. 2:5–11).

2. *The Words of Jesus.* In John 6:63, Jesus says "the words that I have spoken to you are spirit and are life." This statement points out the very close connection between His words and the Spirit. The Spirit dwells in the words of Jesus and uses them in persuading men to accept Christ. The Spirit is not limited to the words of Jesus, but all that He does is in harmony with these words. Because the Spirit is in them, the words of Jesus communicate life.

3. *The Spirit Empowers Believers.* All who proclaim the Gospel should be encouraged to know that the Spirit of God will do His work when we speak. When we proclaim the gospel, we are not just ministering in our own strength. The Spirit of God will draw people to Christ. Several passages of Scripture support this.

First, Jesus, who was empowered by the Spirit, became the baptizer in the Spirit (Acts 1:4–5). As Peter states: "Therefore having been exalted to the right hand of God, and having received from the Father the promise of the Holy Spirit, He has poured forth this which you both see and hear" (Acts 2:33). Jesus baptizes believers in the Holy Spirit to make the believers to be effective witnesses. Jesus declared, "but you will receive power when the Holy Spirit has come upon you; and you shall be My witnesses both in Jerusalem, and in all Judea and Samaria, and even to the remotest part of the earth" (Acts 1:8). When the Holy Spirit is upon us, we become persuasive witnesses.

Second, this theme continues in Acts 2:17–21. Peter repeats God's promise to pour out His Spirit upon all flesh. Although both believers and unbelievers will feel the impact of this, it is the believers that God will use to persuade others to follow Christ. When the Spirit is poured out upon the believers, they will prophesy. Through prophecy, the believers will exalt God and witness. As the end time comes, there also will be great signs and wonders. These cosmic happenings will strengthen the witness of the believers. The result will be that many will call upon the name of the Lord. When they do, they will be saved.

Third, the apostle Paul spoke about the empowerment of the Spirit in his own ministry. Paul declared, "for our gospel did not come to you in word only, but also in power and in the Holy Spirit and with full conviction; just as you know what kind of men we proved to be among you for your sake" (1 Thess. 1:5).

Another passage that has to do with the power of the Spirit in Paul's ministry is Romans 15:18–19. The apostle always kept in focus what Christ had done and his need for the empowerment of the Spirit. Paul wrote:

> [18]For I will not presume to speak of anything except what Christ has accomplished through me, resulting in the obedience of the Gentiles by word and deed, [19]in the power of signs and wonders, in the power of the Spirit; so that from Jerusalem and round about as far as Illyricum I have fully preached the gospel of Christ.

The Spirit's Inner Voice

The Holy Spirit works within the hearts of those to whom we minister. They hear, sense, and feel the inner wooing of the Spirit. Many people who have come to Christ testify to how the Spirit drew them to commit their lives to Christ. Very often, this drawing force is described as the quiet, but strong, voice of the Spirit.

1. *The Impact of Prophecy.* Paul recognized the role of the Spirit in his comments to the Corinthians. Speaking about prophecy, which is a gift of the Spirit, he wrote: "But if all prophesy, and an unbeliever or an ungifted man enters, he is convicted (*elegchetai*) by all, he is called to account by all; the secrets of his heart are disclosed; and so he will fall on his face and worship God, declaring that God is certainly among you" (1 Cor. 14:24–25). When people hear the prophetic words, they will be "convicted" and they will turn to God. Spirit empowered prophecy has a strong impact on the hearers.

2. *God Opens Hearts.* At Philippi, Paul was speaking to some women who had assembled. Concerning Lydia, Luke says that "the

Lord opened her heart to respond to the things spoken by Paul" (Acts 16:14). As a result, Lydia and her household were baptized. Although Luke does not mention the Spirit, the preaching of the Word is clearly a powerful tool in the hands of the Spirit. We can safely conclude that Paul was empowered by the Spirit to speak persuasively to Lydia.

3. *The Spirit Invites.* Revelation 22:12–17 is a fascinating passage that is relevant to our study of the persuasive work of the Spirit. According to verse 17, "The Spirit and the bride say, 'Come.' And let the one who hears say, 'Come.' And let the one who is thirsty come; let the one who wishes take the water of life without cost."

Sometimes this passage is called "the invitation." Actually, the verse includes four invitations. One, the Spirit and the bride, which is the body of Christ, say "Come." Two, the one who hears says, "Come." These two invitations can refer to the call of the Spirit and the body of Christ for Jesus to return (Rev. 22:12), but many hold that they refer to invitations to the world to come to Jesus. Three, an invitation is given to the thirsty to come to Christ. Four, an invitation is given to whoever wishes to take the water of life without cost. The last two invitations are uniformly held to be directed to the world. My view is that all four invitations are to the world. To hold otherwise introduces an abrupt transition from inviting Christ to return to inviting the world to believe in Christ. So the Holy Spirit, as well as the bride, persuasively invites the world to come.

4. *Resisting the Spirit.* Many people resist the work of the Spirit. As an example, when Stephen spoke to the religious leaders before He was martyred, they resisted what his message to them. Stephen confronted them with this declaration: "You men who are stiff-necked and uncircumcised in heart and ears are always resisting the Holy Spirit; you are doing just as your fathers did" (Acts 7:51). When people resist, the resistance is an evidence that the Spirit is attempting to persuade them. Otherwise, there would be nothing to resist. Throughout history, millions of people have rejected Christ and the wooing of the Spirit. Nevertheless, we must keep on witnessing.

Convincing the World

The most extensive passage about the persuasive work of the Spirit is in John 16:8–11. Indeed, we could call this the "classic" passage. It draws together many aspects of the role of the Spirit in drawing people to Christ. In this passage, Jesus declared:

> [8]And He, when He [*the Helper*] comes, will convict (*elegxei*) the world concerning (*peri*) sin and righteousness and judgment; [9]concerning (*peri*) sin, because (*hoti*) they do not believe in Me; [10]and concerning (*peri*) righteousness, because (*hoti*) I go to the Father and you no longer see Me; [11]and concerning (*peri*) judgment, because (*hoti*) the ruler of this world has been judged."

The Spirit, or Helper, will come (John 16:7) and convict the world. "Convict" is an English translation of the Greek word *elegxei*. The same Greek verb is used in 1 Corinthians 14:24. Both the English and the Greek words can have several related meanings. Among other things, these words can mean to find a person guilty, to awaken a consciousness of guilt, to reprove someone of wrongdoing, and to expose what is wrong. At a minimum, to convict (*elegxei*) means to persuasively present the truth. The Helper uses the truth to persuade people to follow Christ. Thus, the term "convince" is an apt description of what the Spirit does. Within the same context, the Spirit is known also as the Spirit of Truth (John 16:13).

With this as background, we will study verses 8–11. The Spirit will convince the world (v. 8) of sin, righteousness, and judgment. Each of these topics (vv. 9–11) is followed by the conjunction *hoti*. One common lexical definition of *hoti* is the word *because*. Another possible translation, which is helpful in explaining these verses, is *seeing that* or *inasmuch as*.

As we examine this passage, we will use both meanings. The word *because* suggests a reason why the Spirit convicts. The phrase *inasmuch as* brings into focus truths that the Spirit uses, or points He is making, to bring about the needed conviction. Both meanings illuminate this passage and are significant for us.

1. *Concerning Sin.* In verse 9, Jesus says that the Spirit will convict (convince) the world "concerning sin, because [*hoti*] they do not believe in Me." As the optional translation, we can read, "*inasmuch as* they do not believe in Me." We will comment on a couple of points.

First, let us begin with the reason why the Spirit convinces. He convicts and convinces *because* men do not believe. The world does not believe the words of Jesus about Himself nor the words of others about Jesus. Thus, the persuasive work of the Spirit is needed. The Spirit has to enlighten, persuade, and convince men that Jesus is the Christ, the Son of God.

Second, in a sense, the clause about sin *defines* what sin ultimately is. The Spirit convicts *inasmuch as* sin is unbelief. Jesus is the Son of God and the unique Savior of the world. Faith in Christ is the only way to be freed from sin. The ultimate sin, the one which will keep us from salvation, is unbelief. All other sins culminate in this sin.

The world has difficulty accepting that they must be saved through faith. Early in His earthly ministry, when speaking to Nicodemus, Jesus made this plain. He said: "He who believes in Him [Christ] is not judged; he who does not believe has been judged already, because he has not believed in the name of the only begotten Son of God" (John 3:18). The Spirit powerfully presents this truth to the lost. In so doing, He persuades them to believe in Christ. All other sins are forgiven when one comes to Christ. When people believe, they are saved.

Millions of people are locked in spiritual darkness. Many have never heard the truth. Others are blinded by Satan and do not accept the truth. Our responsibility is to tell them the truth. As we do, the Spirit will persuade them. Let us testify to the reality of Christ in our lives. He is alive! He has delivered us from sin and forgiven us! He has changed us! The Spirit will use our testimony to persuade others to come to Christ.

2. *Concerning Righteousness.* In verse 10, Jesus declared that the Spirit will convict the world "concerning righteousness, because [*hoti*] I go to the Father, and you no longer behold Me." Here, Jesus is talking about His righteousness. When He was on earth, Jesus lived a perfectly righteous life. He was without sin.

First, let's consider the reason why the Spirit would convince men of Christ's righteousness. When Christ went away, men no longer had His visible example. Thus, *because* Jesus has gone away and they no longer could behold Him, it would be the role of the Spirit to convince men of the righteousness of Christ.

Second, there are convincing truths that stand out in connection with this verse. The Spirit convicts concerning righteousness *inasmuch as* these truths prevail. Let us now consider several of these truths.

One, when Christ completed His atoning work, His righteousness was more fully revealed. We have the example of the righteousness of Christ on earth, but His righteousness was even more fully expressed through His death, burial, and resurrection. Only Christ was sinless. Only He could atone for all others. Only He could pay the penalty for sin. All of this became fully known as Christ completed His work before going away.

Two, through Christ's atoning work and resurrection, the righteousness of Christ became available to all who believe in Him. When we believe in Christ, we participate in His righteousness. We become a part of the body of Christ. We are "in Him" and, therefore, by position as sons of God, we are righteous. This righteousness, except in an anticipatory way, was not possible before the atoning work of Christ was completed.

Three, the personal righteousness of Christ was vindicated by His ascension to the right hand of God. The Holy Spirit had a part in the resurrection (Rom. 1:4) of Christ, His ascension (Heb. 9:14), and His vindication. The apostle Paul mentions these themes in 1 Timothy 3:16 where he states:

> He who was revealed in the flesh,
> Was vindicated in (by) the Spirit,
> Beheld by angels,
> Proclaimed among the nations,
> Believed on in the world,
> Taken up in glory.

The *Paraclete* uses all these truths to persuade men to believe. As the Spirit of truth, He is well armed with truth to persuade men of Christ's righteousness. It is that righteousness that is ours when we come to Christ.

The Helper, in His new role, would not come until Jesus went away. The Holy Spirit was already at work in the lives of men, but His greater work as a witness would come when Christ finished His atoning work. Because of this fact, Jesus regarded the coming of the Helper as an advantage for people. He said, "But I tell you the truth, it is to your advantage that I go away; for if I do not go away, the Helper shall not come to you; but if I go, I will send Him to you" (John 16:7).

Today, we live in a world of pluralistic values. Although some of the values are acceptable; others are not. Even when they are, the failure of men to live up to those values is commonly known. Man, by himself, is incapable of living up to the ideals he himself holds. Let us believe in Christ, accept His righteousness, and begin to live as Jesus would. Our testimony to the righteousness of Christ will be stronger as we live by His precepts. When others see Christ in us, our witness will be strong.

3. *Concerning Judgment.* In verse 11, Jesus declares that the Helper will convince the world "concerning judgment, because [*hoti*] the ruler of this world has been judged." Here, Jesus puts the spotlight on Satan as the ruler of this world. We will focus on two points that are suggested by the conjunction *hoti*.

First, *because* the prince of the world, who is the devil, has been judged, the Holy Spirit will speak convincingly about judgment. At the cross, God judged and defeated the devil through Christ (Col. 2:15). Although the devil has been judged, he still has power. He is still the god of this age (2 Cor. 4:4), but ultimately he will be put away. For Satan, there is no way out of his predicament. However, for the unbelievers there is, through Christ, a way of escape. It is the work of the Spirit to point men to Christ who will deliver them from the judgment.

Second, the judgment suffered by Satan is an illustration of the judgment that will be meted out to his followers. *Inasmuch as* Satan has been judged, His followers will be, too. As a result of the solidarity between the devil and his followers, the followers will be judged just as Satan is judged. Concerning unbelievers, Jesus said, "You are of your father the devil, and you want to do the desires of your father" (John 8:44). The followers of Satan will be judged because of their evil deeds. Concerning the result of that judgment, John writes, "And if anyone's name was not found written in the book of life, he was thrown into the lake of fire" (Rev. 20:15).

We, as believers, will be judged as well. Believers, too, will be judged for their works, but they are righteous in Christ. When we are in Christ, our salvation will not be in question. We can offer to the world the salvation that will deliver them from the consequences of their sins. In contrast to the future for the unbeliever, the future for the believer is bright and full of hope. These are powerful truths that ought to draw the entire world to Jesus. He alone is their Savior.

Conclusion

As we conclude this chapter, our hearts are full of gratitude to God for His saving grace. We stand in awe at the atoning work of Christ, our Lord. We recognize that the Holy Spirit has drawn us to Jesus. He has been the Powerful Persuader in our lives. He has illuminated our minds with the Word of God and has drawn us inwardly to the One who can redeem us from our sins. The work of the Spirit has been transforming and comprehensive in our lives.

Moreover, we are full of faith because we know that, when we witness, the Holy Spirit is at work in His wonderful way to persuade men and women to come to Jesus in faith. We are not alone in our efforts to fulfill the Great Commission. We are working with God Himself. Our God is seeking out the lost and is welcoming them to come to Jesus. He will help us find all those who will respond in faith to Christ. This gives us great hope that our mission, under God, will be accomplished.

CHAPTER THREE
BECOMING SONS OF GOD

One of the most amazing facts of the gospel is that, when we come to faith in Christ, we become sons of God. We become sons by position, and our status in Christ is constant. As sons of God, we have eternal life and become heirs with Christ of all of the benefits of the kingdom of God. Given the awesome possibility of being a son of God, we are intensely interested in how this happens.

Salvation is a result of the work of the Triune God. The Father, the Son, and the Holy Spirit all are involved in the salvation of men. Notice the involvement of all three, for example, when Paul says, "For through him [Christ] we both have our access in one Spirit to the Father" (Eph. 2:18). The believer's personal relationship is with all three Persons of the Trinity. Although all three Persons are involved, our primary purpose in this chapter is to study the role of the Holy Spirit in making us sons of God.

When people believe in Christ, they are united with Christ and are indwelt by the Holy Spirit. Union with Christ and the indwelling of the Spirit constitute a double gift to the one who believes in Christ. The Holy Spirit not only indwells the believer, but He also is involved in all aspects of the believer's union with Christ. One important aspect of His work is to impart to us the assurance that we are the sons of God.

Basic Premises

Our thoughts in this chapter are based on several very relevant premises. These basic premises provide a framework for our teaching concerning the role of the Holy Spirit in the process of believers becoming sons of God. The premises themselves are derived from an inductive study of the appropriate passages in the Word of God.

1. *Our Position.* When we say that we are sons of God, we are referring to our position or status in the mind of God. We actually become His sons and have all the rights and privileges that relate to

that position. When we become sons, then we have the responsibility to live as sons. We do this through a developing relationship with God.

2. *Objective and Subjective.* When we think about our salvation, we must take into account both the objective works of the Spirit as well as our experiential relationship with Him. By "objective" works, I mean that these works are done in the mind of God. Through His objective works, the Holy Spirit lays the foundation for all of our subjective experience. Initially, these works are not experiential, but they establish our position in Christ as sons of God. As we live for Christ, we are blessed with the subjective aspects of the Spirit's work.

3. *The Issue of Sequence.* When we consider union with Christ and reception of the Spirit, the issue of the sequence of salvation elements arises. For example, some scholars hold that reception of the Spirit is logically subsequent to union with Christ. In my view, our initial reception of the Spirit is objective and coordinate with union with Christ.

All of the objective aspects of salvation are followed by subjective experience. To be sure, the subjective experiences may begin right away, but they are ongoing and continuous. Our subjective experience of the Spirit is subsequent to the objective aspects of salvation.

4. *Indwelling and Reception.* When we believe in Christ, the Spirit indwells us. He takes up His abode within us. He dwells within. The term "receive the Spirit" puts the emphasis on our attitude when He indwells. Through faith, we invite the Spirit to dwell within us. Although there are nuances of thought between "indwell" and "receive," these terms can be used somewhat interchangeably. Unless otherwise noted, we will do so in this chapter.

The New Testament Pattern

A major point in how we become sons of God is the New Testament pattern with regard to coming to faith and reception of the Spirit. An examination of the biblical data yields three steps that result in the indwelling of the Spirit: listen, believe, and receive.

1. *Listen.* The work of the Spirit in bringing men to faith in Christ is recognized by Paul. When the Spirit begins His work, men may or may

not be conscious of His activity. At some point, they listen to the message of truth (Eph. 1:13). Through such means as prophecy (1 Cor. 14:24) and the powerful presentation of the gospel (1 Thess. 1:5), the Spirit speaks persuasively to men's hearts. Gradually, or sometimes immediately, men begin to consciously accept what the Spirit says and does.

However, Paul does not use the term *reception* to describe the Spirit's persuasive work. Until a person has come to faith, Paul does not say that either the Spirit or His work has been received. It is not necessary to distinguish sharply between the Spirit and His work in persuasion. However, it is the agency of the Spirit rather than the reception of the Spirit that is stressed in speaking about the Spirit's persuasive work.

2. *Believe.* The process of coming to faith culminates in a person truly believing in Christ. The Holy Spirit lifts up and exalts Christ. Saving faith is not just faith; it is faith in Jesus Christ. The atoning work of Christ is the basis upon which all spiritual benefits are given and received. Until one hears the gospel (Rom. 10:14), he cannot believe. A person can believe as he hears the gospel, but not before. When a person believes, he begins to rely on Christ intellectually, emotionally, and volitionally. It is at this time that he is united with Christ and becomes a part of the body of Christ.

3. *Receive.* When a person believes, the way is opened for him to receive the Spirit. As far as any explicit statements are concerned, Paul always presents the reception of the Spirit as following faith (Gal. 3:2; Eph. 1:13). It is through faith in Christ that the Spirit is received. When a person believes in Christ, the Spirit comes to dwell within him. With regard to the initial reception, which is an objective event, there is no lapse in time. In an experiential sense, the reception is subsequent to the objective moment.

Upon believing in Christ, as Paul says in Ephesians 1:13, we "were sealed in Him with the Holy Spirit of promise." The metaphor "sealed" is flexible and broad enough to include all aspects of the Spirit's presence and work. It does not refer to just a one-time event. Our initial reception of the Spirit is, therefore, a part of being sealed. Other moments in our experience manifest this sealing as well.

Other passages support the view that faith is the doorway to receiving the Spirit. In other words, faith in Christ is a prerequisite. We cannot receive the Spirit without faith in Him. Several key passages from John, Paul, and Luke reveal this pattern.

- John (7:39) declared, "But this He [Jesus] spoke of the Spirit, whom those who believed in Him were to receive; for the Spirit was not yet *given*, because Jesus was not yet glorified."

- Paul said (Gal. 3:2), "This is the only thing I want to find out from you: did you receive the Spirit by the works of the Law, or by hearing with faith?"

- Peter concluded his sermon on the Day of Pentecost with this exhortation, (Acts 2:38): "Repent, and each of you be baptized in the name of Jesus Christ for the forgiveness of your sins; and you will receive the gift of the Holy Spirit."

4. *Order of Salvation.* During the Reformation, much theological attention was devoted to developing an "order of salvation." The order of salvation is concerned primarily with the logical, not the chronological, order of the elements of salvation. It describes the process by which the work of salvation, accomplished through Christ, is subjectively realized in the lives of sinners who become believers. This includes the works of the Holy Spirit in applying the work of redemption.

During the Reformation, a great controversy existed over election and free will. This was, without doubt, one of the main catalysts for the development of the order of salvation. Entirely different orders of salvation result from the sides taken in this debate. The issue was much argued and continues to be a critical element in theology today.

It is not my purpose to develop a full order of salvation. However, a key point in this debate is whether regeneration precedes faith or faith precedes regeneration. Based on the above evidence, my view is that faith comes prior to regeneration. Our regeneration is a work of the Spirit. This does not mean that the Spirit is not at work bringing men to faith, but the regenerating work of the Spirit follows faith. Others hold that regeneration precedes faith.

The Double Gift

When we believe in Christ, we receive a double gift—union with Christ and reception of the Spirit. We might say two gifts, but they are so interrelated that it helps to view them as two aspects of a single gift. We will discuss these two aspects briefly and then turn our attention to 1 Corinthians 12:13, which is a key passage with regard to this subject.

1. *Union with Christ.* Paul repeatedly declares that believers are "in Christ" (Rom. 6:11; 8:1–2; 2 Cor. 5:17; Eph. 2:13; Col. 2:11–14). Also, Christ dwells in the believer (John 14:20; Rom. 8:10; Gal. 2:20; Col. 1:27). It is through faith that we are "in Christ," so faith is the doorway to union with Christ. As a result of our union with Christ, our sins are put to His account, and His righteousness is granted to us. All of the benefits of being sons, including fellowship with Him, are ours.

Several passages illuminate further our union with Christ. According to Ephesians 1:4, God chose us "in Christ." Because we are "in Christ," we are the sons of God. When we believe, we are made alive (Eph. 2:5) together "with Christ." Moreover, as Paul writes in 1 Corinthians 6:17, "But the one who joins himself to the Lord is one spirit *with Him*." Putting all of this together, we have an excellent picture of our union with Christ.

2. *Reception of the Spirit.* As indicated above, reception of the Spirit follows faith. We receive the Spirit in an objective sense upon believing. As a result of this reception, along with union with Christ, we become sons of God. Subsequent to this, we receive the Spirit in an experiential sense because we are sons of God (Gal. 4:6).

In Romans 8:9, Paul declares, "But if anyone does not have [*echei*] the Spirit of Christ, he does not belong to Him." Here, Paul uses a present tense which expresses the importance of a current relationship. However, his statement also takes one back to the point of origin of his Christian life. It can be deduced from the statement that anyone who belongs to Christ has the Spirit. Without the Spirit, you do not belong to Christ.

The passage implies that, when we believe in Christ, we are indwelt objectively by the Spirit. Then, as we live for Christ, we enjoy an experiential relationship with the Spirit. The objective side of salvation saves us from a purely experiential and subjective approach. Our subjective experience gives us great assurance of salvation and the joy of relating in a personal way to Almighty God.

Also, note that Paul uses the title "Spirit of Christ" for the Holy Spirit. The Spirit and Christ are two Persons of the one Godhead. The Spirit and Christ are different yet the same. When one is present, in some sense the other is present. Thus, union with Christ and reception of the Spirit is a twofold gift. Through this twofold gift, we become sons of God.

3. *Key Verse*. A central verse in connection with the above double gift is 1 Corinthians 12:13. Paul declares, "For by [*en*] one Spirit we were all baptized into [*eis*] one body, whether Jews or Greeks, whether slaves or free, and we were all made to drink of one Spirit."

Grammatically, many interpretations of this verse are possible. The first clause has two Greek prepositions, *en* and *eis*, that can be translated in more than one way. The preposition *en* can mean *in*, *with*, or *by*. Therefore, as far as the Greek words and grammar are concerned, we may say that all believers were baptized either "in" or "by" the Spirit. The other preposition is *eis*, and it can mean *into*, *unto*, or *with reference to*. Given this information, we could say that all were baptized "by" one Spirit "into" one body or "in" one Spirit "unto" one body. In the second clause, the Greek verb *epotisthēmen* can mean "made to drink" or "given to drink."

Beyond grammar, some scholars connect the first clause with baptism in water. However, there is nothing in the language or the context that calls for this connection. Thus, our comments below are based on views that do not include water baptism. Even if baptism in water is included, the flexibility of the language does not change. Without dealing with all the various views, I will present my understanding of the passage.

In my view, the first clause refers primarily to union with the body of Christ. This is, in effect, union with Christ Himself. Therefore, a natural reading is that "by" one Spirit, we were all baptized "into" one body. Indeed, this is how the NASB[95] translates the clause. However, we would have about the same result by reading "in" one Spirit we were all baptized "unto" one body. Given the fact that the Spirit is present in His works, there is little difference. The second clause, as I see it, refers to our reception of the Spirit. Either "made to drink" or were "given to drink" is acceptable, but "given" is more in harmony with Paul's terminology.

The language is flexible. Thus, the first clause may include also a reference to a united, empowered, and well functioning body of Christ. Therefore, we could read the clause like this, "in" one Spirit we were all baptized "with reference to" one functioning body. We could even say that "by" one Spirit we were all baptized "into" one united and empowered body. As indicated above, the grammar allows for various interpretations.

Both clauses of this verse are flexible enough to encompass both the objective and the subjective aspects of our relationship with the Spirit. In other words, union with Christ and reception of the Spirit begin with the objective work and presence of the Spirit, but our experiential relationships with Christ and the Spirit develop over time. We need not limit this verse either to the beginning of the Christian life or to its ongoing unfolding.

When we interpret this verse, it helps to realize that the Holy Spirit is, at the same time, both an agent and a gift. When the Spirit acts and does His saving work, He is acting as an agent. When the Spirit indwells us, He is a gift. However, the Spirit is present in His works, and His works are gifts as well as His presence. Therefore, we do not need to distinguish sharply between the Spirit as agent and as gift.

The Works of the Spirit

When a believer is united with Christ and indwelt by the Spirit, several works of the Spirit take place. The believer is regenerated, justified, sanctified, and adopted. We note, also, that the Spirit is present in the works that He performs.

I would say, without attempting to build an order of salvation, that all these works begin in response to faith. To the extent that they are objective, they begin at the same time. With regard to the believer's subjective experience, this happens over time in varying ways.

1. *Regeneration*. Theologically, the term "regeneration" has been used by some to include the entire process of salvation. Others limit the term to the initial moment of salvation. Either way, a change in our moral nature and the impartation of new life are included. Usually, in evangelical theology, the impartation of new life is the specific focus of regeneration.

When people believe in Christ, our Triune God makes them alive and gives them life. The Father is involved in making men alive (Eph. 2:5). Christ, as a life-giving Spirit, (1 Cor. 15:45), gives life to the believer. The Spirit, too, gives life (John 6:63; 2 Cor. 3:6). Those who believe receive the "washing of regeneration" and "renewing by the Holy Spirit" (Titus 3:5–6). When we are "born again," we receive eternal life (John 3:5).

Some scholars hold that regeneration is instantaneous. As such, it would not be experiential because experience requires time. However, as we commonly use the term, especially in the narrower sense, regeneration refers to a subjective experience. This subjective experience has both a definite beginning and an ongoing realization.

2. *Justification*. The Spirit has a role in justification. As in regeneration, the three Persons of the Godhead are involved. The believer has the righteousness from God (Phil. 3:9) on the basis of faith in Christ. He or she is justified by the grace of God (Rom. 3:24) and the blood of Christ (Rom. 5:9). The Spirit is involved as well since the believer was "justified in the name of the Lord Jesus Christ, and in the Spirit of our God" (1 Cor. 6:11).

As the Reformers understood justification, it is objective, forensic, and positional. As an initial act of God, the term "justification" refers to the believer's position in Christ. It is a term that has to do with our standing before God. Because we are justified, we do not have to pay the penalty for sin; we are restored to God's favor, and God considers us to be righteous. This, however, does not alter the need to become righteous in our experience.

In recent times, some scholars have suggested that there is another side to justification. According to them, being "put right" with God involves a subsequent total change in our moral behavior. We are not justified by our behavior, but justification results in a new life. This does not, in their view, do away with the biblical distinction between justification and sanctification. Others, of course, do not believe that justification is in any way a process.

3. *Sanctification.* Another aspect of the saving event is sanctification. As with regeneration and justification, all three Persons of the Godhead are involved. To the Thessalonians, Paul expressed this wish, "Now may the God of peace sanctify you entirely" (1 Thess. 5:23). Paul says, in 1 Corinthians 1:30, that Christ became "sanctification" to us. In 1 Corinthians 6:11, Paul says that we were sanctified, as well as justified, "in the name of the Lord Jesus Christ, and in the Spirit of our God." According to Romans 15:16, we are "sanctified by the Holy Spirit."

Sanctification includes separation to God, being purified from evil, and the righteousness of Christ being imputed to us. The word "impute" means to "reckon" or to "charge to one's account." In other words, when the holiness of Christ is put to our account, we are sanctified in the sight of God. Through sanctification, we are made to conform to the image of Christ (Rom. 8:29). This is the ultimate goal for each of us.

Whether or not the initial moment of sanctification includes any actual moral transformation is debated. According to some scholars, both initial sanctification and the process are concerned with the actual change effected in man. In my view, the initial moment of sanctification is primarily positional, but this does not preclude moral transformation. The process of sanctification is primarily a matter of ongoing inner transformation.

4. *Adoption.* Adoption is another aspect of salvation. One's adoption has to do with being placed as sons of God (Rom. 8:15, 23; 9:4; Gal. 4:5; Eph. 1:5). The apostle Paul regarded Old Testament believers as children but also as minors. New Testament believers are "children" but also "adult sons." Through Christ, we are adopted in the sense of being adult sons of God. An advantage of being a son is deliverance from the law (Gal. 4:3–5). The believer's adoption, when he or she comes to faith, is judicial, but the standing of being a son has an impact on all of our experience. When the bodies of believers are redeemed (Rom. 8:23), adoption has an experiential aspect.

It is God the Father who "predestined us to adoption as sons through Jesus Christ to Himself" (Eph. 1:5). Both the Father and the Son have a part in making the adoption possible (Gal. 4:1–7). In Romans 8:15, Paul says, "you have received a spirit of adoption as sons by which we cry out, 'Abba! Father!'" Although the emphasis of this passage is on the Spirit who makes believers conscious of their sonship, one cannot exclude the role of the Spirit in making them sons and daughters. The Spirit clearly has a part in the future realization of adoption, the redemption of their bodies (Rom. 8:11, 23). This leads one to believe that the Spirit had a part in the adoption when men come to faith as well.

Already–Not Yet

A central concept in the theology of Paul is that some things have "already" happened, but they have "not yet" been fully consummated. The tension between what has already happened and what is yet to be realized applies to all aspects of salvation. One's salvation is in three tenses—past, present, and future. When individuals first believed in Christ, they were saved; now they are being saved; and they will be saved.

The concept of "already–not yet" applies to one's reception of the Spirit Himself. The Spirit draws individuals to Christ. Upon coming to faith in Christ, they are indwelt objectively by the Spirit. A relationship with the Spirit begins, and they are immediately eligible for a highly experiential reception of the Spirit. The believer's experience with the Spirit is ongoing, continuous, and punctuated with special intense moments.

1. *Pledge*. The apostle Paul uses the term "pledge" to describe the Holy Spirit in Ephesians 1:14 and in 2 Corinthians 1:22 and 5:5. As commonly used in the papyri, a "pledge" is earnest money and is a down payment on the total obligation. As Paul uses the term, the purpose of the down payment is to give assurance of the future inheritance. It is a guarantee of what is to come.

In Ephesians 1:14, Paul says it is the Holy Spirit "who is given as a pledge of our inheritance, with a view to the redemption of God's *own* possession, to the praise of His glory." The verb "given" does not appear in the Greek text. Literally, the text reads, "who is a pledge." The Holy Spirit is described as the down payment on one's future spiritual inheritance. The Spirit is a part of the inheritance. This is not to say that the future inheritance will be obtained apart from the Spirit. The Holy Spirit has a part in bringing all spiritual blessings to believers.

In 2 Corinthians 1:22, Paul writes that God "gave us the Spirit in our hearts as a pledge." Similarly, in 2 Corinthians 5:5, he says, God "gave to us the Spirit as a pledge." In both verses, Paul refers to "the earnest, or down payment, of the Spirit." The phrase can mean "the Spirit as a down payment" or the "down payment" of the Spirit with the full inheritance of the Spirit coming later. Unless one drives a wedge between the Spirit and one's full salvation, the two approaches have essentially the same result. The Spirit, now and in the future, is the agent of the works of salvation. Moreover, by metonymy, the Spirit may stand for the whole of salvation. On the whole, in these two passages, the "Spirit as a down payment" is preferable.

This raises a question of timing. Was the Spirit, as a pledge, given at the initial moment of salvation, or subsequently? In my view, believers receive the earnest of the Spirit when they came to faith. However, their consciousness of His presence and assurance may not have been very discernible. Because of this, the consciousness of His function as an earnest may have come later. In an experiential sense, one may consider that the earnest is given to believers when they have this consciousness. The purpose of the earnest is to give assurance of one's future inheritance. Thus, the continuing presence of the Spirit is included.

2. *First Fruits*. According to Paul, "We ourselves, having the first fruits of the Spirit, even we ourselves groan within ourselves, waiting eagerly for *our* adoption as sons, the redemption of our body" (Rom. 8:23). Here, Paul uses the phrase "first fruits of the Spirit."

One way to interpret this phrase is that, by "first fruits of the Spirit," Paul refers to the Spirit Himself. In other words, the "first fruits" are the Spirit. This view distinguishes between the presence, or Person, and the works of the Spirit. Believers have received the Spirit as the "first fruits," and they will receive or realize the full benefits of the Spirit's work in salvation in the future. Another interpretation is that individual believers receive the "first fruits of the Spirit" now and will receive Him in a more perfect way in the future. This view does not distinguish as sharply between the presence and works of the Spirit. The Spirit, who is received at the beginning and in the future, is always at work in the lives of the believers. The end result of these two approaches is about the same.

As I understand the passage, the second view is better. The term "first fruits" is a term related to harvest. The first fruits are a part of the harvest; the rest of the harvest will be of the same kind. Both the first fruits and the entire harvest are the Spirit Himself. This harvest of the Spirit includes all His works on behalf of believers. In this context, His works include the believers' future resurrection (Rom. 8:11) and their adoption as sons (Rom. 8:23).

3. *Hope*. As sons of God, we have hope. In Galatians 5:5, Paul said: "We through the Spirit, by faith, are waiting for the hope of righteousness." As believers, we already have righteousness. We are righteous in Christ and share in His righteousness. Nevertheless, there is a greater fulfillment. Righteousness is still something that is hoped for and awaited. Paul expresses this wish, "Now may the God of hope fill you with all joy and peace in believing, so that you will abound in hope by the power of the Holy Spirit" (Rom. 15:13). Once again, we see the "already–not yet" approach of the apostle Paul.

Conclusion

In this chapter, we have focused on "becoming sons of God." We can rejoice in the fact that, through faith in Christ, we have the position of a son of God. Throughout our lives, we have the joy of an experiential relationship with God. We interact with the Father, Son, and Holy Spirit as sons and servants of our Lord. Our relationship grows, develops, and is enriched as we walk with Him.

When we believe in Christ, we receive the double gift of union with Christ and reception of the Spirit. This double gift is bestowed in an objective sense. As we live with Christ, our experience of Christ and the Spirit develops. All of this gives us a growing sense of assurance that we are sons of God. As the apostle Paul says, "And because you are sons, God has sent forth the Spirit of His Son, into our hearts, crying, 'Abba! Father!'" (Gal. 4:6). God is our Father, and we are sons of God.

CHAPTER FOUR

GIVING AND RECEIVING THE SPIRIT

A crucial element in biblical interpretation is the definition of terms. With regard to the Holy Spirit, we have a strong interest in knowing how the terms having to do with the dispensing and appropriation of the Spirit are defined. The Bible does not use the terms "dispensing" and "appropriation," but these terms are very good when we want to include all of the biblical terms on this topic.

The terms "giving" and "receiving" the Spirit are biblical terms, and they can be interpreted narrowly or broadly. These terms can be used in a broad sense to include all the others having to do with the dispensing and appropriation of the Spirit. It is God who gives the Spirit, while it is the believers who receive Him. Various terms are used by the biblical authors to signify the Spirit being given and received. Although these terms can be used broadly, we still need to examine what they mean in any given passage. The meaning in specific passages may be narrower.

Through an inductive study of the biblical terms with regard to dispensing and appropriating the Spirit, it becomes clear that the language is dynamic and flexible. This is not surprising in that the biblical authors wrote with different purposes over many years. Many controversies arise when we attempt to be too narrow and rigid in using the biblical terms. The temptation is to choose one meaning and to make all other uses conform to that meaning.

The Verbs Used

As we begin this chapter, we will list many of the verbs used by Luke, Paul, and John concerning the Spirit plus the noun "anointing." In a few cases, we will mention other authors as well. These terms are listed in our Table of Terms at the end of this chapter. The terms are listed alphabetically. The lexical form of the Greek terms is used. Our list is not intended to be exhaustive with respect to the verbs used or the references included. We have, however, listed most of them.

General Observations

The language used by the biblical authors concerning giving and receiving the Spirit is rich and varied. The words used include various parts of speech. Nouns, verbs, prepositions, adverbs, and adjectives are all included in the portrayals of the presence and works of the Spirit. However, we will focus on the verbs. With regard to the verbs, various tenses are used. Based on inductive study, we can make the following observations.

1. *Similarities and Differences*. There are similarities and differences in the various terms used by the biblical authors concerning giving and receiving the Spirit. They are similar in that all of them have to do with our relationship with the Spirit. In other words, at the core, words are used that signify our personal connection with the Spirit. However, these terms are not totally synonymous. The differences have to do with the purposes of the authors and the aspects of the relationship with the Spirit that are emphasized. The terms can be used in a variety of contexts.

2. *Metaphors*. Many of the terms used to signify giving and receiving the Spirit are metaphors. A metaphor is a figure of speech that makes an implied comparison between two things that are not alike but which have something in common. For example, Jesus called those who follow him "sheep." We are not literally sheep, but we act much like sheep in our discipleship.

Metaphors are divided into "living" and "dead" metaphors. The living metaphors still retain the original imagery of the metaphor. Over time, metaphors tend to lose that meaning and simply have a meaning different from the original. At this point, they do not rely for meaning on the original object. Dead metaphors can have a meaning different from the original. The dividing line between the two can be hazy and may depend on culture and usage. If the metaphor is living, more can be drawn from it by analogy than from a dead metaphor.

When interpreting metaphors, the question arises as to how much of the original imagery applies to the usage of the metaphor. For example, when we discuss being "filled" with the Spirit, the imagery calls to mind filling a container with some liquid. The Holy Spirit, however, is a Person, not a liquid. So the "liquid" aspects of the imagery do not apply. The phrase "filled with the Spirit" has to do with the influence of the Spirit in our lives.

Metaphors are known to be very flexible. With regard to giving and receiving the Spirit, the metaphors simply express various aspects of our relationship with the Spirit. To a degree, they can be used interchangeably. However, being interchangeable does not mean that they are identical in every respect. Each metaphor has its own nuance of meaning and adds something to the meaning of the relationship.

3. *Multiple Moments.* Believers have a living relationship with the Holy Spirit. Therefore, many of the terms used to describe the relationship are applicable to multiple moments in time and experience. The term "filled" illustrates the point. This term includes the continuous and repetitive nature of the filling of the Spirit. Rather than limiting Paul's terms to one moment or another, it is better to understand one's relationship with the Spirit as alive, ongoing, and punctuated by wonderful moments along the way.

Similarly, the language allows for both the objective and subjective aspects of salvation. For example, Paul says in Romans 8:9, "If anyone does not have [*echei*] the Spirit of Christ, he does not belong to Him." Here Paul uses the present tense. We must have the Spirit now, currently, or we do not belong to Christ. However, this verse implies that the Spirit indwelt us in an objective sense at the beginning of our Christian life. In other words, we can reason our way back to the beginning. What we have already been given in an objective sense, we continually experience in our walk with Christ. Moreover, our experience itself is constantly renewed, developed, and enriched.

The Emerging Picture

As we review the verbs listed in the Table of Terms, several points stand out. One is that some terms are uniquely used by each author— Luke, Paul, and John. Others are used by two of them or all three. Out of our study, we see a common picture as well as the specific emphases of each of the authors.

These verbs paint an amazing verbal picture. Through faith, we come to Christ and we receive the Spirit. The Spirit is poured upon us, and we are regenerated and renewed. By the Spirit, we are washed, justified, and sanctified. We have the Spirit, and without Him we are not Christ's. The Spirit abides in us and will never leave us. Moreover, the Spirit comes upon us, falls upon us, and fills us with power to be witnesses and to serve. We are sealed and anointed with the Spirit. We are baptized by and in the Spirit.

This is the picture from a distance. We might say that this is an aerial view. When we get closer to the ground, closer to each verse, then various interpretations arise. It is then that the specific meanings of each word become important. However, despite these differences in interpretation, one thing is commonly understood. Our relationship with the Spirit is intended to be comprehensive, strong, dynamic, and vital. The Holy Spirit dwells in us and empowers us for all aspects of life and witness.

The Common Core

There are several terms that we might call the "common core" of the thoughts of Luke, Paul, and John concerning the Spirit. The verbs "give" and "receive" are used by Luke, Paul, and John. Luke and Paul use the verb "anoint," and John uses the noun "anointing." Both Luke and Paul use the term "filled." John does not, but he does speak about "rivers of living water." Luke, Paul, and John use the verb "baptize." All three employ the verb "send," which is an English translation of more than one Greek verb.

These terms are widely used among us as believers. Various aspects of these terms are often debated. Also, in some cases, there is considerable agreement among scholars and believers as a whole. Below, we will discuss these terms, the ways they are used, and some of the issues surrounding them. We will hold our discussion of "baptize" until chapter 8.

1. *Send.* Both the Father and the Son are senders of the Spirit. On resurrection evening, Jesus told his disciples, "I am sending forth [*apostellō*] the promise of My Father upon you" (Luke 24:49). Before He departed from earth, Jesus spoke about the Helper, "whom I will send [*pempsō*] to you from the Father" (John 15:26). In John 16:7,

Jesus said, "I will send [*pempsō*] Him [the Helper] to you." Much later, Paul wrote: "And because you are sons, God has sent [*exapesteilen*] the Spirit of His Son into our hearts, crying, 'Abba! Father!'" (Gal. 4:6).

2. *Gives.* The verb "gives" can be used to include all of the verbs that have to do with the dispensing of the Spirit. However, here we will restrict our discussion to the cases where the verb "gives" is actually used. The references include the following

First, we note that God the Father (Luke 11:13; Acts 5:32; 11:17; 15:8; 2 Cor. 1:22; 5:5; Eph. 1:17; 1 Thess. 4:8; John 3:34; 14:16, 1 John 3:24; 4:13) gives the Spirit. According to Paul, God "gave" us the Spirit in our hearts as a pledge (2 Cor. 1:22; 5:5) of our full inheritance. The inheritance involves the Spirit and His works. We know that God abides in us by the Spirit whom He "has given" to us (1 John 3:24; 4:13). Luke states that God "has given" (Acts 5:32) the Spirit to "those who obey Him." Here, Luke uses the present participle *peitharchousin.* Another translation would be "are obeying" Him. All this does not preclude His giving of the Spirit to us in the future. Writing to believers, Paul prayed that God "may give" (aorist subjunctive) you a spirit of wisdom and revelation" (Eph. 1:17).

Second, Jesus also gives the Spirit. Jesus declares that He shall give water to believers that shall become a well of water springing up into eternal life (John 4:14). At a minimum, the term "water" refers here to the Holy Spirit. In passages using other terms, Jesus is named as the sender (John 14:26; 15:26) of the Spirit. Matthew (3:11), Mark (1:8), Luke (3:16) and John (1:33) all mention that Jesus is the baptizer in the Spirit. The relationship between the Father, the Son, and the Holy Spirit is very close and inseparable.

Third, sometimes the verb "gives" is used in the present tense. This means that the giving of the Spirit is not a one-time event. We receive the Spirit continually in our lives. Consider the following relevant passages:

The apostle John writes, in John 3:34, "for He gives [*didōsin*] the Spirit without measure." The verb "gives" is a present tense and represents continual and repeated giving. Several interpretations of this verse are advanced by commentators. It can mean that God gives the Spirit to His Son without measure. Or, it can mean that the Son gives the Spirit to believers without measure. Another view, though less likely, is that the Spirit does not give by measure. As I understand the text, the view that God gives His Spirit to the Son without measure is best.

In 1 Thessalonians 4:8, Paul writes: "So, he who rejects *this* is not rejecting man but the God who gives [*didonta*] His Holy Spirit to you." The people who reject the sanctification that God provides are rejecting God who gives us His Spirit. The verb "gives" is a present participle. It possibly could include a reference to the experiences of separate individuals in succession, but I believe it refers to the ongoing experience of each individual believer. God continues to give each believer His Spirit in abundant measure. We can rejoice in having His powerful and loving presence in our lives.

3. *Receives*. God gives His Spirit to those who believe in Christ. All of the terms used for dispensing the Spirit imply that the believer to whom the Spirit is given does something in response to the gift. The only term that specifically identifies that response is "receives." The believer receives the Spirit that God gives to him. Or, to put this another way, the Spirit indwells the believer, and the believer receives the Spirit. This means that the believer opens his heart and mind to the relationship with the Spirit that God wants us to have. The believer reaches out and joyously accepts the gift from God. Several points about this reception are important.

First, the term "receive the Spirit" can refer to the union of our spirit with the Holy Spirit. The Spirit, in this reception, indwells the believer. Initially, this gift is positional and non-experiential. There is not much direct biblical evidence to support the idea, but it is implied by Scriptures such as Romans 8:9. Without having the Spirit, one cannot belong to Christ. It is our conviction that this indwelling is a gift that comes to us when we believe in Christ. Some commentators hold that the union of our spirit with the Spirit of God is the exclusive meaning of "receive the Spirit." If this were the only meaning, then reception could happen only once. However, this view overlooks the evidence for repeated and ongoing reception of the Spirit.

Second, subsequent to the initial indwelling, the believer receives the Spirit in an experiential way. Because experience takes time, it has to be subsequent to the initial, objective indwelling. Many scholars agree that receiving the Spirit can be, and often is, highly experiential. When believers receive the Spirit, they sense the presence of God. Something great happens within, and they know that God is present with them. Receiving the Spirit is not just a doctrinal position; it is, in many cases, an actual knowable experience.

Third, our experience of the Spirit begins upon coming to faith, but the term is not limited to one moment. The verb "receive" is flexible enough to include initial reception of the Spirit, ongoing and continuous reception, and repeated moments of receptivity. As I mentioned earlier, God constantly gives (1 Thess. 4:8) the Spirit to the believer. What He constantly gives, we receive in an ongoing way.

In John 7:39, John spoke of the Spirit which the disciples "were to receive." John 7:37–38 breathes ongoing experience. The words "thirsty," "come," "drink," and "believes" are all in the present tense. Moreover, the metaphor of the "rivers of living water" suggests continuity of experience. This verse can mean that, in an ongoing way, God gives the Spirit to the believer, that the Spirit flows through the believer to others, or both. If the Spirit continuously flows through the believer, then the believer also receives continuously.

On Resurrection Sunday evening (John 20:22), Jesus breathed on the disciples and said, "Receive the Holy Spirit." Notwithstanding many scholarly efforts to deny that this was a full New Testament reception, my view is that it was. The disciples received the Spirit that evening and, of course, later on the Day of Pentecost.

In 1 Corinthians 2:12, Paul indicates that we have received "the Spirit who is from God that we may know the things freely given to us by God." The Spirit will help us know and understand better the things of God. Although this verse surely includes the reception of the Spirit at the beginning of our Christian life, the language by itself does not limit the reception of the Spirit to just one moment. According to Galatians 3:5, God "provides (*epichorēgōn*, present participle) you with the Spirit and works miracles among you." God provides the Spirit in an ongoing way. What He provides, we receive.

Paul declares that "you have received a spirit of adoption by which we cry out, 'Abba! Father!'" (Rom. 8:15). As in 1 Corinthians 2:12, this passage points to the beginning of our walk with Christ, but receiving the Spirit is not limited to that moment. In Romans 8:23, Paul says that we who have the first fruits of the Spirit are "waiting eagerly for our adoption as sons." The future adoption is a work of the Spirit, just as the beginning was. We have received the Spirit as the first fruits of the harvest. The rest of the harvest is of the same kind. We will receive the Spirit and his work in our future adoption.

Fourth, our reception of the Spirit has an impact on all aspects of our walk with Christ. In Galatians 3:2, Paul asks, "Did you receive the Spirit by the works of the Law, or by hearing with faith?" Later in this chapter (3:14), Paul declares that Christ redeemed us "so that we might receive the promise of the Spirit through faith." These passages are not limited in their scope.

In the book of Acts, reception of the Spirit normally has to do with empowerment to witness and authentication of faith. Jesus told the disciples that they would "receive power when the Holy Spirit has come upon you" to be witnesses (Acts 1:8). The new believers at Samaria (Acts 8:15, 17, 19) received the Spirit. Their reception of the Spirit was an authenticating moment. Similarly, when the disciples at Ephesus had an experiential reception of the Spirit, it was a step forward in their journey with Christ. Paul asked the disciples (Acts 19:2), "Did you receive [*elabete*] the Holy Spirit when [having believed] you believed [*pisteusantes*, having believed]?" The apostle was asking an experiential question—have you received the Spirit in an experiential way? When Paul laid hands on them, they had this experience.

At least two passages in Acts have wider application. When Jesus was exalted to the right hand of the Father, He "received the promise of the Holy Spirit" (Acts 2:33). We could not limit this to only the empowerment aspect of the Spirit's work, but empowerment is included. Jesus poured out the Spirit on the Day of Pentecost. Another crucial passage is Acts 2:38. Peter exhorted the people to repent and be baptized in the name of Jesus Christ. Then, they "shall receive the gift of the Holy Spirit." In my view, Peter at least had in mind the kind of experience the disciples had on the Day of Pentecost, but we may apply this to all aspects of the Spirit's presence and work.

4. *Filled*. Both Luke and Paul use the term "filled" with the Spirit. Although John does not, he does speak about "rivers of living water" (John 7:38). The rivers of living water, in my view, can flow either from Christ to the believer, from the believer to others, or both. John explicitly says (John 7:39) that the "rivers of living water" refer to the Spirit.

First, unlike the term "receive" the Spirit, most scholars agree that the term "filled" with the Spirit is used of more than one moment, as well as continuously, in the life of the believer. A few would disagree, but not many. The evidence for this is strong.

All the disciples were "filled" with the Spirit at Pentecost (Acts 2:4). Later, when Peter was speaking to the rulers and elders, Luke describes him as being "filled" with the Spirit (Acts 4:8). After speaking to the rulers and elders, Peter and John went to their own companions to report what the chief priests and elders had said. During this meeting, "they were all filled with the Holy Spirit, and began to speak the word of God with boldness" (Acts 4:31). At least some of them had been previously filled with the Spirit. One can be filled on repeated occasions, and it is possible to be continually filled.

In Acts 13:52, Luke says that the disciples "were continually filled with joy and with the Holy Spirit." Here, Luke uses the imperfect passive (*eplērounto*) of the verb *plēroō*. The word *plēroō* is the verbal form of *plērēs* (full). Grammatically, this verb in the imperfect tense can be interpreted "filled again and again," "filled one after another," or "kept on being filled." All of these interpretations are possible. For example, we can be continually full of the Spirit, yet be filled again for a special occasion.

The only other such usage of *plēroō* is in Ephesians 5:18. There Paul exhorts, "And do not get drunk with wine, for that is dissipation, but be filled with the Spirit." Grammatically, "be filled" can mean "be repeatedly filled" or "be continuously filled." There is no contradiction between these two meanings. Although we can be repeatedly filled, we may also be continuously filled. Furthermore, we sometimes use the word "continuous" to include repetitious action that happens on a regular basis.

Second, in Ephesians 5:18–19, Paul uses the term "filled" with the Spirit in a broader way than Luke. He exhorts them to be filled with the Spirit, "speaking to one another in psalms and hymns and spiritual songs, singing and making melody with your heart to the Lord, always giving thanks for all things in the name of or our Lord Jesus Christ to God, even the Father." As in Luke's case, Paul lists vocal results of being filled with the Spirit, but the vocalization extends to worship.

Then, in verse 21, Paul says, "And be subject to one another in the fear of Christ." In the verses that follow, Paul lists some ways that we can be subject to one another. Here, being filled with the Spirit results in the manifestation of moral and ethical qualities. Although Paul uses the term "filled" primarily of congregational worship, the influence of the Spirit impacts all of our lives.

5. *Anoint.* With regard to the Holy Spirit, one of the terms that Christians of all backgrounds commonly use is "anoint." In various contexts and with different meanings, we speak about being "anointed" by or with the Spirit. We speak about an anointing for a given ministry or task. This carries with it the idea of being called, appointed, and enabled for that task. Also, we speak about being anointed in a given service or when preaching a sermon or singing a song. Sometimes the anointing is accompanied by great emotions; at other times, we quietly sense the presence of the Spirit.

The word "anoint" is used a few times in the Bible in connection with the Holy Spirit. Although Christians use the term more widely, it is useful to consider the way it is used in the Word. Consider the following instances:

First, Jesus was anointed with the Spirit. Jesus was anointed in the sense of being appointed and empowered. Isaiah 61:1 is a prophetic reference to the Messiah who says:

The Spirit of the Lord God is upon me.
Because the Lord anointed me
To bring good news to the afflicted,
He has sent me to bind up the brokenhearted,
To proclaim liberty to captives
And freedom to prisoners.

In Luke 4:18, Jesus applied this reference to Himself. Again, in Acts 10:38, Peter declared that God "anointed" Jesus "with the Holy Spirit and with power." As a result, Jesus went about doing well and healing all who were oppressed by the devil. In Hebrews 1:9, the writer states that God anointed Jesus with "the oil of gladness." This appears to be a reference to the Spirit. Without mentioning the Spirit, Luke says in Acts 4:27 that God anointed His "holy servant Jesus."

Second, the term "anoint" is used by John in two places with regard to believers. In 1 John 2:20, John says that believers have an "anointing from the Holy One." Then, in 1 John 2:27, he writes about the abiding anointing that we have received. As I understand these verses, the anointing is the Holy Spirit who abides in the believers and teaches them. This abiding presence begins when people come to faith in Christ and continues throughout their walk with Him.

In 2 Corinthians 1:21–22, Paul writes, "Now He who establishes you with you in Christ and anointed [*chrisas*] us is God, who also sealed us and gave us the Spirit in our hearts as a pledge." The Greek verbs translated "anointed," "sealed," and "gave" are all aorist participles. These aorist participles do not determine when these actions took place. Neither do they limit the action to one moment in time.

This is the only time Paul uses the term "anoint." The anointing and the sealing are not done apart from the gift of the Spirit. We are anointed and sealed with the Spirit. The term "anointed" is broad enough to include all aspects of the Spirit's presence and work from initial indwelling to subsequent moments of teaching and empowerment. We should not limit the applications of the term.

Other Terms

Some terms are uniquely used by Luke, Paul, and John. Others are used by two of the three authors. The three writers demonstrate both unity and diversity with regard to the Holy Spirit. They complement each other in giving us a wonderful picture of the presence and work of the Spirit.

1. *Luke and Paul*. Luke alone uses the verbs "fall upon" (Acts 8:16; 10:44; 11:15) or "come upon" (Acts 1:8; 19:6). These verbs describe the Spirit's empowering of the believers to witness and to serve.

Luke's emphasis on empowerment for prophetic witness is the dominant theme of his historical record. He is recording the history and growth of the church. Luke uses the verb "pour out" (Acts 2:17, 18, 33; 10:45) with regard to the Spirit's empowerment. Paul uses it more comprehensively in Titus 3:6.

Altogether, Luke uses seven terms to describe the event at Pentecost. Each of these terms has its own nuance of thought, but they are all used of Pentecost. The terms are "give" (Acts 11:17; 15:8), "baptize" (Acts 1:5; 11:16), "come upon" (Acts 1:8), "fell upon" (Acts 11:15), "receive" (Acts 1:8; 2:38; 10:47), "poured forth" (Acts 2:33) and "filled" (Acts 2:4). Normally, as in Acts 2:4, Luke uses the word *pimplēmi* for "filled;" but in Acts 13:52, he uses the related word *plēroō*. Both these words are derived from the Greek stem *plē*. Luke does not use any other terms in Acts to describe the giving and receiving of the Spirit to the disciples.

2. *Paul, John, and James.* Both John and Paul use the verb "to seal" (John 3:33; 6:27; Eph. 1:13–14; 2 Cor. 1:22; Eph. 4:30). Paul is the main user of the verb "dwell" (Rom. 8:9, 11; 1 Cor. 3:16; 2 Tim 1:14). However, James (4:5) speaks about the Spirit that God "has made to dwell" in us. Paul says that believers (Eph. 2:22) "are being built together into a dwelling of God in the Spirit." Both John and Paul use the verb "have" (1 John 2:20; Rev. 3:1; Rom. 8:9, 23; 1 Cor. 6:19; 7:40; 2 Cor. 4:13). As noted above, Paul, as well as Luke, uses the verb "pour out."

3. *John.* John alone uses the Greek term *menō*, which is translated as "remain" and "abide." He recorded that the Spirit "descended" upon Jesus and remained (John 1:32–33). According to John, the Spirit abides (John 14:17; 1 John 2:27) in us. The Holy Spirit (Helper) will be with us forever (John 14:16). As indicated above, both John and Paul use the verb "have." In 1 John 3:9, John refers to God's seed that "abides" in the believer. The "seed" can refer to the Spirit, the Word, or both.

As we study the doctrine of the Holy Spirit, we need to pay attention to all that is recorded in the Bible. This will include the writings of Luke, Paul, and John. John is the most comprehensive with regard to what Jesus said. He deals with life, truth, maturity, and ministry. Many scholars have studied the similarities between Luke and Paul, but not as many have compared Luke and Paul with John. More work should be done on this subject.

Expositors have noted Luke's emphasis on empowerment for service and prophetic witness. Similarly, many have observed Paul's emphasis on salvation terms. Given these observations, the contrast between Luke and Paul is drawn between their themes of empowerment and salvation. This contrast exists, but it is even more complete to say that Luke's more narrow emphasis on empowerment stands in contrast to Paul's more comprehensive emphasis. The apostle emphasizes all aspects of the Spirit's work, including empowerment and salvation.

Conclusion

The biblical language with regard to giving and receiving the Spirit is amazingly flexible, varied, and rich in imagery. It is a mistake to narrowly define these terms and limit their meaning. When we do, our understanding of many passages is impoverished. Many theological arguments could be resolved simply by more inclusive interpretation of the crucial terms.

When we study all the terms, we see how rich and full our relationship with the Holy Spirit can be. Our relationship begins even before we come to faith in the sense that the Holy Spirit persuades us to believe in Christ. Upon believing, the Spirit indwells us objectively and begins His experiential presence and work in our lives. That presence and work touches every aspect of our being.

TABLE OF TERMS

TERMS	LUKE	PAUL	JOHN	OTHER
Abide (*menō*) Remain			John 1:32, 33; 14:17; 1 John 2:27; 3:9	
Anoint (*chriō*)	Luke 4:18; Acts 4:27; 10:38	2 Cor. 1:21		Heb. 1:9
Anointing (*chrisma*)			1 John 2:20, 27	
Baptize (*baptizō*)	Luke 3:16; Acts 1:5; 11:16	1 Cor. 12:13	John 1:33	Matt. 3:11; Mark 1:8
Come Upon (*erchomai*)	Acts 1:8 (*eperchomai*); 19:6 (*erchomai*)			
Dwell (*oikeō*)		Rom. 8:9, 11; 1 Cor. 3:16; 2 Tim. 1:14 (*enoikeō*)		James 4:5. Made to dwell (*katoikeō*)
Fall Upon (*epipiptō*)	Acts 8:16; 10:44; 11:15			
Filled (*pimplēmi* or *plēroō*)	Luke 1:15, 41, 67; Acts 2:4; 4:8, 31; 9:17; 13:52 (*plēroō*)	Eph. 5:18 (*plēroō*)	John 7:37–39 Rivers of living water	
Give (*didōmi*)	Luke 11:13; Acts 5:32; 8:18; 11:17; 15:8	2 Cor. 1:22; 5:5; Rom. 5:5, Eph. 1:17; 1 Thess. 4:8	John 3:34; 4:10, 14; 14:16; 1 John 3:24; 4:13	
Have (*echō*)		Rom. 8:9, 23; 1 Cor. 6:19; 7:40; 2 Cor. 4:13	1 John 2:20; Rev. 3:1	
Pour Out (*ekcheō*)	Acts 2:17, 18, 33; 10:45	Titus 3:6 ; Rom. 5:5 (love)		
Provide, Supply (*epichorēgeō*)		Gal. 3:5; Phil. 1:19		
Receive (*lambanō*)	Acts 1:8 (power), 2:33, 38; 8:15, 17, 19; 10:47, 19:2	Rom. 8:15; 1 Cor. 2:12; 2 Cor. 11:4; Gal. 3:2, 14	John 7:39; 14:17; 20:22; 1 John 2:27	
Sealed (*sphragizō*)		Eph. 1:13; 4:30; 2 Cor. 1:22	John 3:33; 6:27	
Send (*apostellō*)	Luke 24:49	Gal. 4:6 (*exapostellō*)	Rev. 5:6; John 15:26; 16:7 (*pempō*)	1 Peter 1:12

CHAPTER FIVE
TYPES OF EXPERIENCE

As believers seek to realize all that God wants for them, their experience of the Spirit is varied. Given this variety, one must consider the nature of experience and the types of experience an individual may have. When we realize all that is available, we can live with a strong expectation of personal friendship and relationship through the Spirit with our mighty God.

Nature of Experience

Experience may be defined as something personally encountered, undergone, or lived through. As one thinks about experience, one encounters the related concepts of "consciousness" and "being observable." The Bible does not speak in these terms, but a consideration of them will help define the proper use of the term "experience." It is a term that is widely used in theological discussions as well as in everyday interaction about our relationship with God.

1. *Consciousness*. Broadly speaking, experience may be conscious or subconscious. When experience is subconscious, the individual has no awareness of the events taking place. His faculties are not knowingly exercised. However, in its narrower sense, and in common usage, experience is conscious. When it is conscious, the person with the experience perceives what is happening. He is aware of the exercise of his mental, emotional, and volitional faculties. In theological circles, the term "experience" or "experiential" usually refers to perceived experience. The term "non-experiential" often refers to unperceived experience. Unless otherwise indicated, these terms will be used in their usual theological sense in this study.

2. *Observable*. One can think of experience in terms of "being observable" by others. An individual, of course, can experience things that are unobservable to others. Although others may not know it, the person perceives what he or she has experienced. However, many things that one experiences are observable to others. These things are

called "observable" when others can see or perceive what the individual does or expresses.

The objective works of God are realized over time in the experience of the believers. Our relationship with the Spirit is both individual and collective, and it is full and varied. It is subjective as well as objective. Our relationship with the Spirit is with Him as a Person. It is dynamic and stable, full and focused, exciting and constant, and in every way personal. We will turn now to a discussion of various types of experience.

Quiet Experience

When we believe in Christ, we gain the standing of sons of God. This is our position, and it is accomplished by God's objective works. Our experience begins as well. Through our experience of the Spirit, we realize all that God has bestowed upon us. Our initial experience may be quiet and unnoticed or very intense. For many the intensity comes over time.

1. *Objective Works.* The objective works of God underlie and make possible all of our experience. When we say "objective works," we mean that what is done is an act of God. The works are decisions that He makes. He makes the decisions based on the objective work of Christ in atoning for our sins. It is the objective work of Christ in His death, burial, and resurrection that is the source of all that we experience in Christ. Moreover, it is the objective work of the Spirit that applies the atoning work of Christ to our lives. After the Spirit does His objective work, our experience with the Spirit begins and continues throughout our lives.

Several other points may be made about the objective works of the Spirit. One, the objective works bring about our standing with God as sons. Our relationship with God is based on what He has done and on what His perspective is. Two, we are not conscious of what God does objectively, but we begin to experience the result. If our salvation depended on our being conscious of God's actions, our foundation would be insecure. Our experience, however, certainly strengthens our faith. Three, God's objective acts do not require development over earthly time. However, factors leading to God's decisions may take place over time.

2. *Objective and Subjective.* In a sense, everything that God does in our salvation has an objective as well as a subjective side. His works include union with Christ, regeneration, indwelling of the Spirit, sanctification, justification, adoption, sealing, being baptized in and by the Spirit, and more. The emphasis of these terms varies. The emphasis of regeneration is on subjective experience; justification emphasizes the objective work of God; and sanctification stresses both objective and subjective aspects of salvation. Many agree that sanctification is both positional and progressive.

Jesus speaks about the work of the Spirit in regeneration. The one who believes in Christ is born again. In John 3:5–8, Jesus stresses the result of the regenerating work of the Spirit. It was not the regenerating itself that was so experiential, but it was the result.

Jesus was having a conversation with Nicodemus. Nicodemus wanted to know how a man could be born again. Then Jesus answered (John 3:5–8):

> [5]Truly, truly, I say to you, unless one is born of water and the Spirit he cannot enter into the kingdom of God. [6]That which is born of the flesh is flesh, and that which is born of the Spirit is spirit. [7]Do not be amazed that I said to you, "You must be born again." The wind blows where it wishes and you hear the sound of it, but do not know where it comes from and where it is going; so is everyone who is born of the Spirit.

With regard to verse 8, some writers stress that the Spirit's work is mysterious like the wind. In other words, the Spirit works where and how He wills. No doubt this is true, but the point of the comparison must be looked at as well. Jesus says that everyone who is born of the Spirit is like the wind that blows. Just as we see the result of the blowing wind, we see the result of being born again.

The Holy Spirit is involved in all these works. In 1 Corinthians 6:11, Paul states, "Such were some of you; but you were washed, but you were sanctified, but you were justified in the name of the Lord Jesus Christ and in the Spirit of our God." Initially, these are objective works of the Spirit. However, each of these works develops in the life of the believer in time. For example, the person who comes to faith is judicially justified by God. As he walks with Christ, actual moral change takes place.

3. *Varied Experience.* As our experience of the works of the Spirit begins, it may be almost unnoticed. This is why I have named the initial experience, "quiet" experience. Millions of people come to Christ and begin to serve Him without any initially intense emotional moment. This is often true of children who have been brought up in Christian homes. They accept Christ in a very natural and moral way without much experiential demonstration. On the other hand, there are many others who have a very knowable experience accompanied by intense emotion. Often this is an emotion of great joy and praise. Either response is valid. The crucial issue is that people accept Christ in faith. They believe on Him as Savior. Many times, the emotional responses come later in their experience.

Crisis Experience

Most Christians believe in the value of crisis experiences in our relationship with the Spirit. The crisis experience may take place when a person accepts Christ, perhaps later when God calls the believer to a vocation, in times of prayer when God makes Himself intensely known, and on many more occasions. Even though crisis experiences are highly valued, an issue arises over whether or not reception of the Spirit is a knowable crisis experience. The issue becomes more debatable when we talk about receiving the Spirit more than once.

1. *Valued Experience.* A hallmark of our Pentecostal approach is that we highly value the crisis experience called the baptism in the Holy Spirit. Thus, the classic Pentecostal passage for this type of experience is Acts 2:4. With regard to the outpouring of the Spirit on the Day of Pentecost, Luke writes: "And they were all filled with the Holy Spirit and began to speak with other tongues, as the Spirit was giving them utterance." The disciples were fully conscious of the Spirit's presence; this was a knowable result in their lives. Also, it was an observable experience, known to all who were present. Each person in the multitude heard the disciples speaking in his own language (Acts 2:6).

Similar experiences happened at Samaria, Caesarea, and Ephesus. When Philip preached in Samaria, many people believed (Acts 8:12), but the Holy Spirit had not yet fallen upon them (Acts 8:16). Peter and John were sent from Jerusalem to minister to them. They prayed for the disciples to receive the Holy Spirit. When they laid their hands on the people, they received the Spirit. Simon "saw" (Acts 8:18) that the disciples received the Spirit. It was an observable experience.

A great breakthrough of the gospel came among the Gentiles at the house of Cornelius in Caesarea. Peter spoke to the audience that Cornelius had gathered in his house. The Holy Spirit was poured out upon the disciples. The believing Gentiles had a conscious and observable experience with the Spirit. Luke describes what happened (Acts 10:44–48) as follows:

> [44]While Peter was still speaking these words, the Holy Spirit fell upon all those who were listening to the message. [45]All the circumcised believers who came with Peter were amazed, because the gift of the Holy Spirit had been poured out on the Gentiles also. [46]For they were hearing them speaking with tongues and exalting God. Then Peter answered, [47]"Surely no one can refuse the water for these to be baptized who have received the Holy Spirit just as we *did*, can he?" [48]And he ordered them to be baptized in the name of Jesus Christ. Then they asked him to stay on for a few days.

At Ephesus, Paul met with some new and uninstructed disciples. Observing their need, Paul asked them: "Did you receive the Holy Spirit when you believed?" (Acts 19:2). "When you believed" is a translation of the aorist participle *pisteusantes*. Literally, this participle means "having believed." Thus, the question is "Having believed, did you receive the Holy Spirit?"

Many commentators treat this question as though it were a doctrinal question. However, given the uninformed status of the disciples, it is not likely that Paul was asking them a doctrinal question. It was, in my view, an experiential question. He was asking them if they had received the Spirit experientially. They had not. So Paul instructed them further and prayed for them. Luke writes, **"And when Paul had laid his hands upon them, the Holy Spirit came on them, and they *began* speaking with tongues and prophesying"** (Acts 19:6). They had a conscious and observable experience of the Spirit.

2. *Repeated Reception.* Peter had been filled with the Spirit on the Day of Pentecost, but later he was filled for a special purpose. On the occasion of the healing of the lame man, the rulers and elders were

upset because the apostles were "proclaiming in Jesus the resurrection from the dead" (Acts 4:2). So the rulers and elders inquired, "By what power, or in what name, have you done this?" (Acts 4:7). Peter understood the question to be referring to the miracle that had occurred. Luke says that "Peter, filled with the Holy Spirit," answered them (4:8) saying that the man was healed by the name of Jesus Christ. In this way, Peter was empowered to confront the rulers and elders.

3. *Subsequent Moments*. Clearly, all who come to Christ receive the Spirit, but this does not preclude subsequent moments when the Spirit is received. The apostle Paul wrote about one of those moments in Galatians 4:6 where he states, "Because you are sons, God has sent forth the Spirit of His Son into our hearts, crying, 'Abba! Father!'" God sends His Spirit into our heart in a way that we know the Spirit is present. The Spirit inspires us to cry out to God in adoration and worship as well as in supplication. We receive the Spirit in a very conscious way.

Another fascinating passage is Romans 8:26–27. Many times, we are confronted with situations when we do not know how to pray. It is at times like this that the Spirit will pray through us according to the will of God. The believer clearly has an observable and conscious experience of the presence of the Spirit. Here, Paul writes:

> [26] And in the same way the Spirit also helps our weakness; for we do not know how to pray as we should, but the Spirit Himself intercedes for *us* with groanings too deep for words; [27] and He who searches the hearts knows what the mind of the Spirit is, because He intercedes for the saints according to *the will of* God.

4. *All Experience*. There are two extremes with regard to crisis experiences with the Spirit. One extreme is to minimize their importance. Many believers highly value an ongoing, stable, and growing relationship with the Spirit, but they do not see the value of a crisis experience. In other aspects of life, in connection with other personal relationships, they know that life is enriched by special, memorable moments, but they overlook this in their relationship with the Spirit. Perhaps they doubt the long-term impact of such an experience. The other extreme is to place such a high value on a crisis experience that the ongoing presence of the Spirit is too lightly considered. In any other relationship, we know that there has to be an

ongoing and constant dimension. Friendship endures, grows, and develops. Surely, the right position is to value all our experience with the Spirit, including both the crisis experiences and the ongoing dimensions of our relationship.

Continuous Experience

Many Scriptures support the point that the Spirit abides in us, dwells in us, and is continuously with us. As these passages indicate, we can "know" his abiding presence as well as the special moments of crisis experience. When you know the Spirit's abiding presence, you can live with assurance of your right relationship with God. This is one of the great blessings in our walk with Christ. We will highlight a few Scriptures to illustrate the point.

1. *John*. In John's Gospel, Jesus spoke often about the continuous, ongoing presence of the Spirit. In John 7:39, He said, "from his innermost being will flow rivers of living water." The pronoun "his" does not specify whether the clause refers to Christ or to the believer. So, this clause can be interpreted as water flowing from Christ to the believer or from the believer to the world. In my view, both points are valid. In any case, this is an abiding and abundant presence of the Spirit.

Before Christ went through His atoning work, He spoke to the disciples about the Spirit as the Helper. This Helper (John 14:16), Jesus said, will be "with you forever." He will teach (John 14:26) the disciples all things and bring all things to their remembrance. Moreover, as the Spirit of Truth (John 16:13), He will guide them into all truth. All of this suggests an ongoing and continuous presence of the Spirit.

2. *Luke*. The continuous presence of the Spirit is described by Luke with the term "full." When the church needed men of God to oversee the daily serving of food to the widows, they selected (Acts 6:3) "seven men of good reputation, full of the Spirit and wisdom." Luke says that one of these men, Stephen, was a man "full of faith and of the Holy Spirit" (Acts 6:5). In these cases, an ongoing fullness is suggested. However, the term "full" of the Spirit can refer to special occasions as well. In Acts 7:55, Stephen was blessed no doubt with a special fullness for the occasion. As he was about to be

stoned, he was "full" of the Holy Spirit. He gazed into heaven and saw Jesus standing at the right hand of God.

3. *Paul*. Frequently, Paul writes about the continuous presence of the Spirit in our lives. Indeed, as he declares, without this continuous indwelling presence, we do not belong to Christ. In Romans 8:9–11, he writes:

> [9]However, you are not in the flesh but in the Spirit, if indeed the Spirit of God dwells [*oikei*] in you. But if anyone does not have [*echei*] the Spirit of Christ, he does not belong to Him. [10]If Christ is in you, though the body is dead because of sin, yet the spirit is alive because of righteousness. [11]But if the Spirit of Him who raised Jesus from the dead dwells [*oikei*] in you, He who raised Christ Jesus from the dead will also give life to your mortal bodies through His Spirit who dwells [*enoikountos*] in you.

It is important to note that the verbs "have" (v. 9, *echei*) and "dwells" (v. 9, 11, *oikei*) are in the present tense. The verb *enoikountos* (v. 11) is a present participle. Given the present tense, Paul is referring to current and continuous indwelling of the Spirit. This does not deny the objective work of the Spirit at the beginning of salvation, but it does impress on us the importance of a current vital relationship with the Spirit.

Paul writes about the provision and supply of the Spirit in Galatians 3:5 and Philippians 1:19. Taking these verses together, we have a picture of the Spirit being continuously supplied, thus continuously received. Those who use the term "receive" only in the sense of the union of our spirit with the Holy Spirit greatly impoverish the term.

In Galatians 3:5, Paul rhetorically asks, "So then, does He who provides [*epichorēgōn*] you with the Spirit and works miracles among you, do it by the works of the Law, or by hearing with faith?" The word "provides" is translated from a present participle meaning "providing" or supplying. God's provision of the Spirit is continuous and, in this case, is connected with miracles. However, other aspects of the Spirit's presence are not precluded.

In Philippians 1:19, Paul writes about his imprisonment. He says, "For I know that this will turn out for my deliverance through your prayers and the provision [or supply, *epichorēgias*] of the Spirit of Jesus Christ." By "my deliverance," Paul may mean his victory through the testing, the fact that Christ will be glorified, or his ultimate realization of salvation.

Because Paul did not make one of his planned visits to Corinth, his integrity and reliability were being challenged. He defends his integrity by pointing out that God "establishes us with you in Christ" (2 Cor. 1:21–22). He writes:

> [21]Now He who establishes [*bebaiōn*] us with you in Christ and anointed us is God, [22]who also sealed us and gave *us* the Spirit in our hearts as a pledge.

Here, when Paul says "establishes," he uses a present participle. Therefore, this is a constant and progressive experience. Given this, Paul seems to argue that he could not be anything but trustworthy. Then, as further evidence of His integrity, Paul declares that God "anointed" and "sealed" us and "gave us the Spirit in our hearts as a pledge." All of these terms have ongoing, as well as initial, dimensions.

To the Ephesians (5:18), Paul says, "And do not get drunk with wine, for that is dissipation, but be filled [*plērousthe*] with the Spirit." Paul uses two present tense imperatives, "do not get drunk" and "be filled with the Spirit." These imperatives can refer to repeated action or to continuous action. So, we can interpret Paul as meaning "be repeatedly filled" or "be continuously filled" with the Spirit. Both points are applicable to our walk with Christ.

Measures of Experience

We can experience measures of the Spirit's power and presence. This was true of Jesus, and it is true of us. God gave the Spirit "without measure" to Christ. As believers, we experience the presence and power of the Spirit in varying degrees or measures. No matter what we have experienced, we always can experience more. Our infinite God will bestow on us what we need at any given time.

1. *Jesus.* With regard to Jesus, John writes: "For He whom God has sent speaks the words of God; for He gives the Spirit without measure" (John 3:34). The first clause, "He whom God has sent,"

refers, I believe, to Jesus. Jesus was uniquely both the message of eternal life and the predicted messenger of the New Covenant (Mal. 3:1).

Given this, we have two potential views of the second clause. It could mean that the Father gives the Spirit to the Son without measure or that the Son gives the Spirit to believers without measure. Through purposeful ambiguity, John may have included both truths. God gives the Spirit to Jesus; Jesus gives the Spirit to believers. However, the view that God gives the Spirit to Jesus is stronger. Four reasons support this. One is that the purpose of the passage is to exalt Christ and His witness. Two is that this view harmonizes with verse 35 where God explicitly has given all things into Christ's hands. Three, it is in Jesus alone that the Spirit is seen in the fullest measure. Four, although John speaks about Christ being the giver of the Spirit, this comes later in the story.

The writer says "without measure." "Without measure" is a *litotes* for "in complete fullness." A *litotes* is a way of understating a truth. This truth is expressed by stating the negative of the contrary. The Spirit is given negatively without measure but positively in complete fullness. Also, we note that "gives" is a present tense. This indicates that the giving of the Spirit is not a one-time event, but it is continual.

2. *Believers*. Although, as believers, we will not ever experience the unlimited measure of the Sprit's presence that Christ enjoyed, we can be filled to overflowing with an abundance of the Spirit's presence. The life of Christ represents the ideal standard of experience for us. We want to experience the Spirit in as full a measure as possible. Several passages of Scripture illuminate the concept of measures of the Spirit's presence.

In Titus 3:5–6, Paul wrote, "He [God] saved us, not on the basis of deeds which we have done in righteousness, but according to His mercy, by the washing of regeneration and renewing by the Holy Spirit, whom He poured out upon us richly through Jesus Christ our Savior." As I understand the passage, the term "poured out" can be used inclusively to include one's entire relationship with the Spirit. The Spirit's work includes regeneration, renewal, and empowering for service. The phrase "renewing by the Holy Spirit" emphasizes the ongoing spiritual development of the believer. Clearly, in order to have growth, there must be measures of experience in the Spirit.

In his letter to the Ephesians, Paul prays for their spiritual maturity (3:14–21). In this prayer, he deals with both the indwelling Christ and the indwelling Spirit. He highlights the growth aspect of our experience. Paul prays:

> [16]that He [God] would grant you, according to the riches of His glory, to be strengthened with power through His Spirit in the inner man, [17]so that Christ may dwell in your hearts through faith; *and* that you, being rooted and grounded in love, [18]may be able to comprehend with all the saints what is the breadth and length and height and depth, [19]and to know the love of Christ which surpasses knowledge, that you may be filled up to all the fullness of God.

There is an upward spiral in spiritual maturity. Here, Paul was praying for people who were already believers. When they believed in Christ, they received the Spirit. When they had the Spirit within, they also had Christ. However, as the Spirit strengthens them, they will further experience the presence of Christ through faith. Christ will further dwell in them. Given the close relationship between Christ and the Spirit, a greater indwelling of Christ includes a greater indwelling of the Spirit.

As believers, we are all growing up to the stature of Christ. As Paul says, the spiritual goal for the body of Christ is that we "all attain to the unity of the faith, and of the knowledge of the Son of God, to a mature man, to the measure of the stature which belongs to the fullness of Christ" (Eph. 4:12). Although we will never fully attain His perfect stature, our development can be marked by the ideal of His fullness.

The Holy Spirit has an essential role in this maturation process. By the Spirit, we are being transformed. As Paul says in 2 Corinthians 3:18, "But we all, with unveiled face, beholding as in a mirror the glory of the Lord, are being transformed into the same image from glory to glory, just as from the Lord, the Spirit." The final phrase in this verse indicates the close relationship between Christ and the Spirit. As the Spirit has an impact on our lives, we grow in Christ. We have a greater measure of the Spirit's influence on our lives.

Dimensions of Experience

Believers in Christ experience the Spirit in various dimensions of their relationship with the Spirit. In our studies, we have devoted much attention to the dimensions presented by John, Luke, and Paul. They have different emphases, but in the end they are harmonious and complementary. We will add more detail in our next chapter, but will mention some of the dimensions here.

1. *John.* Among the dimensions stressed by John are eternal life and truth. John says (20:31) "but these have been written so that you may believe that Jesus is the Christ, the Son of God; and that believing you may have life in His name." One of the titles for the Holy Spirit in John is "Spirit of Truth." The Holy Spirit enlightens us and guides us into all truth.

2. *Luke.* The focus of Luke is on the Spirit's empowerment to witness. We learn in Acts 1:8, for example, that the Spirit enables us to witness. Jesus said, "But you will receive power when the Holy Spirit has come upon you; and you shall be My witnesses both in Jerusalem, and in all Judea and Samaria, and even to the remotest part of the earth." Along with this, he stresses the attestation of the believer, revelation of knowledge, dreams and visions, inspired speech, guidance for life and ministry, mighty deeds, and resisting the Spirit. Much of this has to do with the planting, growth, and development of the church.

3. *Paul.* The apostle Paul is very comprehensive in what he presents. Most of what he says may be organized under the headings of life, maturity, ministry, and worship. He deals with the work of the Spirit in our becoming sons of God, including both the objective and the subjective aspects. He puts much emphasis on our maturity in Christ through the Spirit and our worship of God. Also, he stresses Spirit-inspired and empowered ministry.

Conclusion

The picture we get is that our Christian life begins with the objective, non-experiential, acts of God. Immediately, we begin to experience the works of God within and through our lives. The experiences we have may be quiet and almost unobserved, crisis moments of great intensity, continuous presence of the Spirit, experience of the Spirit in various measures, and His presence in many dimensions of the Spirit's life and work. All this adds up to a very rich life in the Spirit, with many aspects of ongoing assurance and special surprise moments of the Spirit's great intervention in our lives. With all of this experience available to us, we can truly count ourselves as beloved sons of God.

CHAPTER SIX

DIMENSIONS OF THE SPIRIT

The authors of the biblical texts include many dimensions of the Spirit's presence and activities. They emphasize the presence and works of the Spirit in connection with their purposes in writing. Here, we will consider the various dimensions that each author stresses. Also, much of our interest surrounds the dimensions of life, maturity, ministry, and worship. We find evidence for all of these dimensions throughout the Bible, but each author deals with them in a different way. Each author enriches the other. This lesson briefly presents some of my findings.

Old Testament

It is important for us to study the Old Testament with regard to the Spirit. We need to know what dimensions of the Spirit are presented in the Old Testament and how the New Testament writers built on what they said.

1. *Old Testament Dimensions.* The Old Testament is quite comprehensive in its treatment of the Holy Spirit. It deals with the contemporaneous experience of the Old Testament saints, prophecies about the Spirit and the Messiah, and the predicted role of the Spirit in the lives of believers.

First, with regard to contemporaneous experience, the primary emphasis is on the Spirit's empowerment and attestation of His people. The Spirit empowers the children of Israel in vocational endeavors, in ministry, and in prophetic speech. Other dimensions are included, but these are the dominant themes.

Second, speaking prophetically, the coming of the Spirit upon Christ is a pronounced theme. The prophecies were fulfilled in the life and ministry of Christ while He was on earth. Christ continues, even now, to relate to us through the Spirit. Christ and the Father are both givers of the Spirit. All who believe in Christ are eligible to receive the Spirit.

Third, as far as believers are concerned, the prophesied role of the Spirit is comprehensive. His presence and work will be evident in imparting new life, in developing the saints in the image of Christ, and in empowering for service. As we study the New Testament, all of these emphases will be present.

2. *New Testament Roots.* The New Testament authors have built on the inspired writings of the Old Testament. We notice this in the writings of Luke, John, and Paul. Although they all had the entire Old Testament as their source, each one had some connections with specific Old Testament writers. As examples, we note the following points.

First, Luke (Acts 2:16–21) draws from Joel (2:28–32) as well as other writers. Moses, for example, wished that all would prophesy (Num. 11:29). Much of the Old Testament emphasis on the empowerment of leaders and prophets carries forward in Luke and Acts. This calls to mind Micah (3:8) who was filled with the Spirit of the Lord to rebuke Israel. Now, all who believe in Christ (Acts 2:38–39) are eligible for the prophesied empowerment.

Second, John emphasizes new life. No doubt he has drawn from the writings of Ezekiel with regard to the life-giving role of the Spirit. In Ezekiel, the Spirit gives both physical life and spiritual renewal (11:19; 36:26–27; 37:5). However, the Spirit's application of the redemptive work of Christ awaited the glorification of Christ (John 7:39). Building on such Old Testament passages, John develops the theme of the new birth (John 3:3–8).

Third, Paul has the most complete coverage concerning the Spirit. He builds on the writings of both Isaiah and Ezekiel. Isaiah wrote comprehensively about the Spirit (e.g. Isa. 32:15–18; 44:1–5). In his writings, he deals with the ethical side of life, social justice, empowerment, the fertility of the land, and the Spirit upon the Messiah (61:1). The Lord, in Ezekiel 36:25, declares that He will sprinkle clean water on the people and cleanse them from all their sins. All this provides background for Paul's writings.

Fourth, the entire New Testament supports the view that we must rely fully on the Spirit of God in all that we do and become. This message is articulated throughout the Old Testament. In Zechariah 4:6, the angel said to Zechariah, "This is the word of the LORD to

Zerubbabel saying, 'Not by might nor by power, but by My Spirit,' says the LORD of hosts." Therefore, the entire Bible fully supports the position that we are fully dependent on the Spirit of God. Without the Spirit, our work will come to naught. With His help and guidance, we can do all that God calls us to do.

Luke's Writings

As far as Luke is concerned, he stresses dimensions that mainly have to do with ministry. He is writing the history of the planting, growth, and development of the church. One of the dimensions is the baptism in the Spirit. We will treat this in a later lesson.

1. *Mission.* Very clearly, Luke connects the Holy Spirit with the mission of the church. Jesus gave the Great Commission, and Luke marshals all the data that show how the disciples were empowered to fulfill the mission. This study examines this issue from two perspectives: (1) Witnesses and (2) Attestation.

First, the terms "mission" and "witnesses" are complementary. "Mission" stresses the purpose, and "witnesses" stresses the action of the disciples. The mission of the witnesses is to present Christ to the entire world. These witnesses include apostles, prophets, teachers, evangelists, and all disciples. What they do can be called missions.

Jesus told the disciples, "You shall receive power when the Holy Spirit has come upon you; and you shall be My witnesses both in Jerusalem, and in all Judea and Samaria, and even to the remotest part of the earth" (Acts 1:8). The book of Acts records the story of how this promise was fulfilled. The mission of the church today has not changed. Believers today, too, are witnesses to the entire globe. Their task is to fulfill the Great Commission. The history of the spread of the Gospel is still being written!

Second, all that the Spirit does attests to the truth of Christianity; but, in several cases, the attestation factor stands out. Not only in the case of John the Baptist, mentioned above, but also Jesus and the disciples were attested by the Spirit.

At Caesarea, the Holy Spirit was poured out upon the Gentiles. They began "speaking with tongues and exalting God" (Acts 10:46). According to Peter, this was sufficient evidence that they were eligible for water baptism (Acts 10:47). Later, at the Jerusalem Council, Peter said, "And God, who knows the heart, testified to them giving them the Holy Spirit, just as He also did to us" (Acts 15:8). The Gentiles were fully authenticated as disciples. This was a huge forward step in the mission of the church.

2. *Inspired Speech.* The fulfillment of the mission of the church comes through both divine and human activity, with the human activity being empowered by the Spirit. From the divine side, the Spirit empowers speech. From the human standpoint, the empowered witnesses, like Moses, were men of "power in words" (Acts 7:22) as well as deeds.

The church is commissioned to spread the Gospel, but not all speech is a direct proclamation. Witnesses are empowered to speak in all situations to meet the need. In some cases, the empowered speech may be considered to be preaching or witnessing or both. Sometimes praise is involved as well. Inspired speech may be studied under the headings of prophecy, speaking in tongues, and other speech.

First, when Peter explained what happened on the Day of Pentecost, he quoted Joel (Acts 2:17–18), declaring that one result of the Spirit's outpouring would be prophetic speech. Peter said, "Your sons and daughters will prophesy." Although Joel does not say so, Peter adds that God's bondslaves will prophesy (v. 18). Prophecy includes messages to God (praise) as well as messages to men. Clearly, Peter saw speaking in tongues as a form of prophecy. The Spirit would be poured out upon all flesh, so that all can prophesy.

Second, in the book of Acts, Luke states three times that the disciples spoke in tongues. With regard to Pentecost, he writes, "And they were all filled with the Holy Spirit and began to speak with other tongues, as the Spirit was giving them utterance" (Acts 2:4). The people in the audience (Acts 2:6), hearing the disciples speaking in their own languages, said, "We hear them in our *own* tongues speaking of the mighty deeds of God" (Acts 2:11).

Third, when Peter and John met with the disciples after this, the disciples prayed for strength to speak the Word of God with confidence. This prayer also included their expression of faith that

God would extend His hand to heal and work signs and wonders in the name of Jesus. Luke then declares, "And when they had prayed, the place where they had gathered together was shaken, and they were all filled with the Holy Spirit and *began* to speak the word of God with boldness" (Acts 4:31).

3. *Guidance*. A very dominant emphasis in Luke, both before and after Pentecost, is on the guidance by the Holy Spirit. Sometimes that guidance included a revelation from the Spirit about relevant circumstances. Today, witnesses are to be guided and led by the Spirit. May believers today always be sensitive to His leadership!

First, the Spirit guided the disciples with regard to decisions affecting their spiritual life (Acts 15:28), the selection and appointing of leaders (Acts 13:2), and the steps to take in ministry (Acts 16:6–10). As an example, consider how God led Peter concerning the Gentiles.

Second, three verses have to do with how the Spirit led Peter with regard to his ministry to the Gentiles at Caesarea. In his vision concerning eating animals (Acts 10:9–16), a voice told Peter, "What God has cleansed, no longer consider unholy" (v. 15). Then, "While Peter was reflecting on the vision, the Spirit said to him, 'Behold, three men are looking for you. But arise, go downstairs, and accompany them without misgivings; for I have sent them Myself'" (vv. 19–20). Then, in Acts 11:12, when Peter was telling the story, he repeated what the Spirit said, stating, "The Spirit told me to go with them without misgivings."

4. *Power and Mighty Deeds*. The Triune God is the source of power. In his Gospel, Luke speaks of the "power of God" (22:69), the "power of the Lord" (5:17), and the "power of the Spirit" (4:14). Also, he writes about the "power of the most High" (1:35), and "power from on high" (24:49). Many times, Luke simply says "power." All three Persons of the Trinity have infinite power.

First, as Luke uses the terms "power" and "Spirit," they are not synonymous. The Holy Spirit has power and manifests power. Very often, it is the Spirit who empowers people with the power of the Triune God. The Spirit is either said to be the source of power or the context yields that information.

Second, Luke mentions that the Holy Spirit empowered Jesus (Luke 4:18; Acts 10:38) to heal and do mighty works. In some instances, Luke does not mention the Holy Spirit in connection with Jesus and his mighty works (Acts 2:22; Luke 5:17), but the Spirit's role in the ministry of Jesus is definite and extensive. Typically, when people were healed under the ministry of the apostles, Luke says they were healed on the basis of faith in Jesus (Acts 3:16; 4:10). However, this does not exclude the power of the Spirit.

5. *Revelation.* One of the key features in Luke–Acts is the work of the Spirit in revelation. This includes His activity in inspiring Scriptures as well as in revealing knowledge to the disciples. Revelation includes the Spirit inspiring Scriptures (Acts 28:25) and the Spirit revealing knowledge (Luke 2:25–26).

First, Luke presents the Spirit as the inspirer of Old Testament Scriptures. He is the revealer of truth. When the disciples were seeking to select a replacement for Judas, Peter cited Psalms 41:9 and 109:8. He said that the Scripture had to be fulfilled, "which the Holy Spirit foretold by the mouth of David concerning Judas" (Acts 1:16). The Holy Spirit spoke, but it was through the mouth of David.

A similar case arose when Peter and John were released from prison. They went "to their own" and reported what had happened (Acts 4:23–31). My thinking is that "their own" included many disciples, not just the inner circle. The assembled believers began praying and cited Psalm 2:1–2. They acknowledged that God had spoken to them by the Holy Spirit through the mouth of David. Once again, the Spirit inspired a message through the mouth of David.

Second, the Spirit reveals knowledge to the disciples. Many times, inspired speech and guidance involved special revelation from the Holy Spirit. As these dimensions are discussed, the author will highlight the moments of revelation. Some Scriptures, obviously, could be listed in more than one category.

Three verses in succession mention the Holy Spirit in connection with Simeon. In Luke 2:25, the Holy Spirit "was upon" Simeon. Next, 2:26 states that it had been revealed to Simeon "by the Holy Spirit" that He would not see death before he had seen the "Lord's Christ." The Holy Spirit revealed a special and personal truth to

Simeon. No doubt his heart was full of joy over this. Finally, in 2:27, Simeon "came in the Spirit into the temple." Simeon goes on to say, "For my eyes have seen Thy salvation" (2:30).

6. *Dreams and Visions.* Dreams and visions were a definite part of the experience of the early church (Acts 2:17; 7:55). These included Spirit-inspired dreams as well as others. As has been seen, the guidance by the Spirit is a strong emphasis in Luke–Acts. Some of the guidance came by means of dreams and visions, through which knowledge is sometimes revealed. Two specific verses connect the Spirit with visions and dreams. Other visions are woven into stories about Cornelius, Peter, and Paul.

First, according to Peter, God says, "I WILL POUR FORTH OF MY SPIRIT ON ALL MANKIND; AND YOUR SONS AND YOUR DAUGHTERS SHALL PROPHESY, AND YOUR YOUNG MEN SHALL SEE VISIONS, AND YOUR OLD MEN SHALL DREAM DREAMS" (Acts 2:17). According to Joel, one of the results of the Spirit's outpouring "in the last days" is that "your young men will see visions and your old men will dream dreams."

Second, other visions are reported by Luke, but they are not directly connected with the Holy Spirit. An angel of God, seen by Cornelius in a vision, spoke to him (Acts 10:3). God spoke to Peter through a vision and a "voice" concerning animals, birds, and crawling creatures (Acts 10:17). In Acts 11:5, Peter says, "I was in the city of Joppa praying; and in a trance I saw a vision, an object coming down like a great sheet lowered by four corners from the sky; and it came right down to me." According to Luke, "While Peter was reflecting on the vision, the Spirit said to him, 'Behold, three men are looking for you'" (Acts 10:19). The Spirit then told Peter to go with them (Acts 11:12).

7. *Other.* The Holy Spirit is mentioned in company with goodness (Acts 6:3), faith (Acts 7:55), joy (Acts 13:52), and wisdom (Acts 6:3). Also, as Luke makes clear, the Spirit can be blasphemed (Luke 12:10), lied to (Acts 5:3; 5:9), and resisted (Acts 7:51). Any experience with the Spirit will have an impact on our moral lives. After all, the Holy Spirit is Holy.

John's Writings

The central themes in John's writings about the Holy Spirit are in harmony with his purposes in the books he wrote. John was concerned about evangelism, discipleship, and community. Given these purposes, we can expect to see that the Spirit is related by him to these themes.

1. *Jesus and the Spirit.* The relationship between Jesus and the Spirit is very close. Jesus is the Person in the Trinity who became incarnate and sacrificed His life for us. He became a divine/human person. Along with the Father and the Holy Spirit, Jesus always existed, but a new relationship was inaugurated in the life and ministry of Jesus on earth. Three key passages in John's Gospel describe the Spirit's coming upon Jesus: John 1:29–34; 3:31–36; and 6:26–27. Because Jesus was man as well as God, it was important for Him to be empowered and attested by the Spirit. Also, Jesus is the baptizer in the Spirit (John 1:33). It is the Father and the Son (John 15:26) who send the Spirit to be our Helper.

2. *The Transition.* The incarnation, life, and ministry of Christ brought a new dimension into human existence. The Spirit of God was present in the Person of Christ. With the birth of Christ, a transition was begun that would not become complete until Jesus was glorified. There was an advance aspect of the Spirit's work because Christ was present, but the consummation awaited the glorification of Jesus (John 7:37–39). The glorification came with His death, burial, resurrection, and ascension. Now that Jesus is with the Father (John 14:16–17; 16:7), the Spirit can fully apply the work of redemption to our lives.

John sometimes uses the present tense when we might expect him to speak of something in the past or in the future. This raises the question as to whether any of the promised future work of the Spirit could have applied in any sense to believers before the glorification of Jesus. The present tense, of course, can be used in various ways. It can be used in the sense of a rhetorical future or to narrate an event that happened in the past. Although, in John's writings, the future is already present to a degree, the future will be greater.

3. *The Presence*. John emphasizes the presence of the Spirit. This presence includes having the rivers of living water flow (John 7:37–39) either from Christ to us, from us to the world, or both. He speaks about the Spirit abiding within us (John 14:16–19; 1 John 2:27; 3:9) and about being "in" the Spirit (Rev. 1:10). All aspects of the Spirit's work are included. He gives life, helps us in many ways, and empowers us for ministry. The Spirit's presence is evidence that we abide in God and He in us (1 John 3:24; 4:13). Moreover, the Spirit's presence assures us of our abiding relationship with Christ.

4. *Eternal Life*. The dominant theme in the Gospel of John is eternal life. So, John very naturally emphasizes the role of the Spirit in giving eternal life. The Holy Spirit works powerfully in our lives to draw us to Christ (John 16:8–11). When people believe in Christ, He radically transforms them through the new birth and the bestowal of eternal life (John 3:5–8). John says (John 6:63) that "It is the Spirit who gives life." Moreover, when Jesus speaks, His words "are spirit and are life." Jesus is the only way to salvation (John 10:1, 9).

5. *Truth*. John is very concerned about truth. He connects all three Persons of the Trinity with truth. Believing the truth is essential to salvation. John calls the Holy Spirit the "Spirit of Truth" (John 14:17; 16:13). John teaches us much about the relationship between the Spirit and truth. The Spirit guides us into all truth (John 16:13), brings truth to our remembrance (John 14:26), and keeps us from error (1 John 4:1–6). Thus, we find that there is a strong connection between the Spirit, the truth, and the Word of God. Also, those who worship God must worship "in Spirit and truth" (John 4:24).

6. *Maturity and Ministry*. John includes the dimensions of spiritual maturity and ministry with regard to the Spirit's work. These emphases are not as strong as some of his other themes, but they are nevertheless included. John's teaching on maturity focuses on the Spirit and Word of God. Believers have an anointing that abides and teaches them (1 John 2:20, 27). The anointing could refer to either the Spirit or the Word. The best approach, I believe, is that the anointing refers to the Holy Spirit in His teaching role. He also deals with the Spirit's empowerment of the disciples in ministry. The disciples were commissioned on resurrection Sunday night to

proclaim the gospel that would call men to repentance and faith (John 20:22–23). Their destiny depended on their response.

7. *The Spirit Speaks.* The Spirit constantly spoke in the Old Testament times, during the ministry of Christ, in the days of the early church, throughout church history, and He still speaks today. John wrote to the seven churches (Rev. 2:1–3:22) in Asia. In each case, John records Jesus' exhortation to the people to listen to the Spirit. The Spirit both warns and speaks comforting words, and the faithfulness of the believers will be rewarded. At the end of the book, the Spirit invites all who will hear to come to Christ, the Savior of the world. There is no salvation in any one else.

8. *Sacramentalism.* Whether or not John took a sacramental approach in his writings is debated among theologians. In my view, he did not. Several passages in John's writings are said to be related to baptism (John 3:5–8; 1 John 5:6–8), the Lord's Supper (John 6:60–65) and worship (John 4:16–26). Although I do not accept the sacramental approach, it is clear to me that the Spirit is powerfully present in these aspects of our experience. Depending on your view, the ceremonies of water baptism and the Lord's Supper may be called church ordinances or sacraments. When Jesus spoke to Nicodemus, the "water" refers, we believe, to the Spirit and perhaps to the Word.

Paul's Writings

The apostle Paul wrote comprehensively about the Spirit, touching on many subjects that relate to our relationship with the Spirit. In my studies, I have focused on Paul's treatment of the Spirit in the life, maturity, ministry, and worship dimensions. These dimensions are not mutually exclusive; they overlap with each other. When the Spirit is present in one dimension, He is to some extent present in all the others.

1. *The Life Dimension.* The Life dimension has to do with a person being drawn to Christ by the Spirit, and the role of the Spirit in regeneration and related aspects of salvation. Various topics are discussed, including persuasion (Rom.10:13–17; 1 Cor.2:4–5; 14:24–25; 1 Thess.1:5); regeneration and renewing (Titus 3:5–7); being washed, sanctified, and justified by the Spirit (1 Cor.6:11); and a

further look at sanctification, new life, and the Spirit in the inner life (Rom. 8:1–13). New life is viewed as both individual and corporate (1 Cor. 1:9).

2. *The Maturity Dimension.* As soon as we receive new life, the process of growing toward maturity begins. Paul presents the goal of maturity, the role of the Spirit in our maturity, putting off the old man and putting on the new man (Col. 3:9–10); the work of the Spirit in instructing us (1 Cor. 2:6–10; Eph.1:17); our walk (Rom.7:6); the fruit of the Spirit (Gal. 5:16–26); assurance of salvation (Rom. 8:14–17); prayer and intercession (Rom. 8:26–27); and prayer for maturity (Eph.3:14–21). The Spirit intercedes in prayer for the believer.

3. *The Ministry Dimension.* Paul emphasizes the ministry of the Spirit, the empowering of the Spirit in word and deed, and spiritual gifts. He deals with spiritual gifts in Romans 12:6–8; 1 Corinthians 12–14; and Ephesians 4:7–13. Also, he speaks about Timothy (1 Tim. 4:14; 2 Tim. 1:6) and his spiritual gift, urging him to exercise it. Paul placed a high value on his own calling (Rom. 15:18–19), and he regarded the ministry as the ministry of the Spirit. To be effective ministers, we must be empowered by the Spirit.

4. *The Worship Dimension.* Just as the Spirit is involved in other aspects of Christian living, so He is involved in worship. Several passages deal with this subject, including Colossians 3:15–17; Ephesians 5:18–21; and Philippians 3:3. In 1 Corinthians 14, Paul discusses several aspects of worship and related matters. He focuses attention on the exercise of spiritual gifts in the worship service.

5. *Realization of the Promise.* Another highly important emphasis in Paul's writings is the realization of the promise. We notice this with regard to terms such as "baptized" (1 Cor. 12:13), "anointed "(2 Cor. 1:21), and "sealed" (Eph. 4:30). The goal for each Christian is to be filled (Eph. 5:18) with the Spirit in all aspects of his life. The Spirit is both an agent and a gift. God supplies the Spirit to the believer (Phil. 1:19), and the believer is being established in Christ. The Spirit is the pledge of our inheritance. We grow in the Lord, and the Spirit (2 Cor. 3:18) shapes us in Christ's image.

Conclusion

The Holy Spirit is the Third Person of the Trinity. He is eternal, infinite, and fully personal. The Spirit extols and exalts Jesus Christ as our Lord and Savior. When we accept Christ, we are united with Christ and indwelt by the Spirit. We could also say that we are united with the Spirit and indwelt by Christ. Because we are, we have a very personal relationship with the Triune God.

Our relationship has many dimensions. Through a study of all of the authors in the Bible, we can recognize a great variety of dimensions that affect our lives. These dimensions are to some extent overlapping. They affect all aspects of our lives. We have no aspect of our lives untouched. Instead, the Spirit has an impact on every detail of our existence. Truly, we are friends, sons, and servants of the great God of the universe. What a privilege is ours! We must keep ourselves open to the realization of all that God grants to us.

CHAPTER SEVEN
ETERNAL LIFE AND TRUTH

In the writings of John, the themes of eternal life and truth stand out. These themes are interrelated in that, to have eternal life, we must have faith in Christ who is the truth. Unless we know and believe the truth, we cannot have eternal life. Given these themes, the role of the Holy Spirit in connection with them is very important in John's writings.

In our last chapter, we mentioned the work of the Spirit in connection with eternal life and truth, but we will discuss these topics more fully in this chapter. The work of the Spirit is not done alone, but rather in cooperation with the Father and the Son. Also, the work of our Triune God is closely connected with His Word. So these connections will be noted as we discuss the role of the Spirit.

Faith in Christ

1. *Purpose*. John clearly states his purpose in writing. He desires that we may have life in Christ, and that life comes through faith in Him. Faith in Christ is the very cornerstone of eternal life, both as it begins and as it continues. Moreover, John wants us to have a strong sense of community in our spiritual lives.

John stresses faith in Christ in his Gospel. In John 20:30–31, he writes a strong purpose statement. Here is what he says:

> [30]Therefore many other signs Jesus also performed in the presence of the disciples, which are not written in this book; [31]but these have been written so that you may believe that Jesus is the Christ, the Son of God; and that believing you may have life in His name.

The tense of the verb translated "may believe" in verse 31 is debated. Early manuscript evidence varies. Some manuscripts use the present tense, while others use the aorist tense. Using the present subjunctive, the verb can be translated as "that you may believe." When the aorist tense is used, the translation may be "that you might come to believe," "that you may keep on believing," or "that you might believe finally and completely." Actually, our initial coming to faith, our continuing to believe, and our ultimate development in faith are strongly emphasized in John's writings. So, any and all of these readings are relevant to our lives. The important point is that John wants us to have faith in Christ.

Similarly, in 1 John 5:13, the author states, "These things I have written to you who believe in the name of the Son of God, so that you may know that you have eternal life." Here the emphasis is on instructing those who already believe. This will result in enriching the lives of those in the believing community. In 1 John 1:3–4, John says:

> ³what we have seen and heard we proclaim to you also, so that you too may have fellowship with us; and indeed our fellowship is with the Father, and with His Son Jesus Christ. ⁴These things we write, so that our joy may be made complete.

2. *Pathway to Eternal Life*. Jesus makes the pathway to eternal life very clear. In John 14:6, He claims that "I am the way, and the truth, and the life; no one comes to the Father but through Me." Moreover, John says, "He who has the Son has the life; he who does not have the Son of God does not have the life" (1 John 5:12). According to John 3:16, "God so loved the world, that He gave His only begotten Son, that whoever believes in Him shall not perish, but have eternal life." Eternal life comes through Christ and through Christ alone. The central truth is that to have eternal life, people must believe in Jesus.

Eternal Life

The Holy Spirit has an essential role in giving both physical life and eternal life. With regard to eternal life, the Spirit is a powerful persuader, drawing people to Christ. In addition, He transforms people through the new birth and gives them eternal life. God gives believers the Spirit to help them in their walk. The presence of the Spirit gives believers great assurance of their salvation. The Spirit influences them in all aspects of their lives. In addition, the Spirit has a role in giving physical life.

1. *The Triune God*. All three Persons of the Trinity have a part in giving eternal life to believers. John's Gospel states that: (1) both the

Father and the Son have life in themselves (5:26), (2) the Father gave His Son that all mankind might have eternal life (3:16), (3) the Son gives life to whom He chooses (5:21), (4) the Spirit gives life (6:63), and (5) those who hear Christ's word and believe in God have eternal life (5:24). Thus, the Word of God also has a role in providing eternal life.

2. *The Spirit's Role.* The Holy Spirit's role in giving eternal life is essential. We have already treated the subject of persuasion in chapter two. The Spirit persuades men to believe in Christ. Beyond this, the new birth is a work of the Spirit, and it is the Spirit who gives life.

First, when people believe in Christ, the Spirit does His work in the new birth. Early in his Gospel (3:5–8), John establishes that all persons must be born again. Jesus proclaims this truth during His meeting with Nicodemus.

> [5]Truly, truly, I say to you, unless one is born of water and the Spirit he cannot enter into the kingdom of God. [6]That which is born of the flesh is flesh, and that which is born of the Spirit is spirit. [7]Do not be amazed that I said to you, "You must be born again." [8]The wind blows where it wishes and you hear the sound of it, but do not know where it comes from and where it is going; so is everyone who is born of the Spirit.

Nicodemus was amazed when Jesus spoke about being "born again." He wondered how a man could be born again when he was old. Jesus addressed his amazement by referring to the blowing wind. Some scholars say that the wind mysteriously blows where it wills and say that the work of the Spirit is similar. This is no doubt true, but the main point of the comparison is that, like the results of the blowing wind, we see the result of the Spirit's work. Through the new birth, we are radically transformed.

Every person's life is formed by heredity, environment, and will. All three have a part in shaping the individual. When Jesus says, "That which is born of flesh is flesh" (v. 6), He stresses one's heredity. A person's natural heredity cannot produce a spiritually transformed life. One's wayward will and the environment further limit the individual. Something new has to take place. This something new is the person's being born of the Spirit. When an individual is born again, he or she has a new heredity!

The issue of the transition between the Old Testament and the New Testament comes into focus in this passage. Jesus was speaking to Nicodemus before He had finished His redemptive work. Was it possible for Nicodemus, at that time, to be born again? Scholars have differing opinions about this. As I see it, it was possible right then for Nicodemus to be born again in anticipation of the redemptive work of Christ. However, when Christ died, was buried, rose again, and was seated at the right hand of the Father, there would be new dimensions to the new birth. The atoning work of Christ would be fully applied to believers when He accomplished His redeeming mission.

Second, at the synagogue in Capernaum, Jesus gives His Bread of Life discourse (John 6:22–59). The discourse gives the true meaning of the miracle Christ wrought in feeding the multitude. The miracle was a sign pointing to Jesus as the Savior of the world. Physical food will perish, but the food that endures to eternal life (6:27) will come through Him.

After the Bread of Life discourse, the disciples reacted. They did not understand and were disturbed by what Jesus said. In 6:60–65, Jesus responded to their concerns. As a part of His response, Jesus gives a key statement about the flesh and the Spirit: "It is the Spirit who gives life; the flesh profits nothing; the words that I have spoken to you are spirit and are life" (v. 63). In a general and unspecified sense, flesh does not give life. Whether a person regards flesh as human nature, literal flesh and blood, or human nature inclusive of literal flesh, it profits nothing. Life is not derived from flesh.

With regard to Christ, He gave His flesh at Calvary. This sacrifice was absolutely necessary for mankind's salvation. The flesh of Christ was interpenetrated by the Spirit of God. His sacrifice opened the way to experience the quickening of the Spirit and the new birth. However, even His flesh by itself does not bring life. It is the Spirit who ultimately gives life.

3. *The Metaphor of Water.* Water is a key metaphor in the thinking of John. As with many metaphors, water can have many

meanings. The interpreter is dependent on the context to help decide what John means. We will consider the meaning of "water" in John 3:5, John 4:10, 14; and John 7:38–39. As we shall see, metaphors have great flexibility in meaning. We are not limited in our understanding to one meaning.

First, just what "water" means in John 3:5 is much discussed. At least four options are included: (1) water baptism, (2) natural birth, (3) the Word, and (4) the Holy Spirit. In my view, along with others, water in this passage is symbolic of the Spirit. However, there may be a secondary reference to the Word. Whatever view is held about water here, the emphasis of the passage is on having faith in Jesus and the transformation wrought by the Spirit of God. Without the Spirit of God, there is no new birth.

Second, consider the meaning of the water metaphor in John 4:7–15. This passage relates the story of the meeting between Jesus and the woman of Samaria who had come to draw water at the well at Sychar. She asked Jesus (v. 7) to give her a drink. Then, in verse 10, Jesus answered and said to her, "If you knew the gift of God, and who it is who says to you, 'Give me a drink,' you would have asked Him, and He would have given you living water." Moments later, Jesus said, "but whoever drinks of the water that I will give him shall never thirst; but the water that I will give him will become in him a well of water springing up to eternal life" (v. 14).

With regard to "living water," the water can be interpreted as (1) spiritual life; (2) the Holy Spirit; (3) Jesus; (4) broadly, to all that leads to eternal life; or (5) with multiple or combined meanings. As I understand this passage, the primary meaning is the Holy Spirit, but other meanings make sense as well. Jesus, His words, and the Holy Spirit all issue forth in life.

The "living water" is abundantly supplied. When "living" applies to literal water, it means "flowing" water as opposed to stagnant water. Moreover, this flowing water is "spring" water that leaps up before you. In a spiritual sense, as Jesus used the term, it means that the "water" leaps up into eternal life. The water of life is abundant.

Third, in John 7:38–39, the metaphor of "living water" clearly refers to the Holy Spirit. Jesus speaks in verse 38, and John adds his comment in verse 39. The passage reads as follows:

> [38]He who believes in Me, as the Scripture said, "From his innermost being will flow rivers of living water." [39]But this He spoke of the Spirit, whom those who believed in Him were to receive; for the Spirit was not yet *given*, because Jesus was not yet glorified.

As John makes clear in verse 39, the "rivers of living water" will flow out of "his" innermost being. As we have elsewhere pointed out, "his" can refer to Christ, the believer, or both. John often speaks, it seems, with purposeful ambiguity.

4. *Assurance of Salvation*. There are many reasons why believers know they are saved. Among them are these four: (1) they know first because the Word of God assures them they are saved through faith in Christ; (2) they know because God has changed their lives; (3) they know because His love is manifested through them; and (4) they know because of the presence of the Spirit in their lives.

In 1 John 3:24 and 4:13, John highlights the role of the Spirit in assurance. In 1 John 4:13, he writes, "By this we know that we abide in Him and He in us, because He has given us of His Spirit." The word "because" is significant. This word introduces a reason why an individual knows that he or she abides in God and God abides in him or her. That reason is clearly stated: Because God "has given us of His Spirit."

God abides in believers, and they abide in God. This mutual abiding presence has a powerful impact on believers' lives. Whatever happens, they know they are directly and intimately related to the almighty and loving God. This should inspire their deepest loyalty and an outflow of love from themselves to others.

5. *Physical Life*. The Spirit has a role, also, in giving physical life. Revelation 11:1–14 presents John's comments on the two witnesses who will prophesy for 1260 days in Jerusalem. When they have finished their testimony, the beast that comes up out of the earth kills them. The people rejoice that the witnesses have been killed. However, the celebration of the unbelieving masses ends soon. After three and a half days, God brings the two witnesses back to life. This

was accomplished (v. 11) by "the breath of life" from God. Another way this phrase can be translated is "Spirit of life." This causes great fear to come upon the masses. The two witnesses stand on their feet, demonstrating that they are alive.

Truth

One of the great themes in John's writings is truth. The purpose of this chapter, with regard to truth, is to examine the passages in John's writings that connect the Holy Spirit with truth. Several points are important to this discussion.

1. *The Triune God*. As in the case of eternal life, all three Persons of the Trinity are connected with truth. In John 3:33, one learns that God is true. Later, Jesus declared, "I am . . . the truth." Repeatedly in John's Gospel, Jesus calls the Holy Spirit the Spirit of Truth (John 14:17; 15:26; and 16:13). Moreover, John says, "And it is the Spirit who bears witness, because the Spirit is the truth" (1 John 5:7). We usually think of the Spirit as the communicator of truth, but He also is the truth.

2. *The Spirit and the Word*. There is a close connection between the Spirit and the Word in John's writings. For example, John says the believer does not practice sin "because His seed abides in him" (1 John 3:9). The pronoun "His" can refer to God or to the Spirit, but the preceding reference to God favors the former. Moreover, the "seed" can be viewed as the Spirit, the Word, or both. It makes little difference whether the seed is regarded as the Word inspired by the Spirit or the Spirit who inspires the Word. Since John has a way of using words with more than one meaning, it could easily be concluded that the seed refers to the Spirit and the Word. In reality, both the Spirit and the Word abide in the believer.

3. *Truth and Eternal Life*. John includes this exchange between Pilate and Jesus: "Therefore Pilate said to Him, 'So You are a king?' Jesus answered, 'You say *correctly* that I am a king. For this I have been born, and for this I have come into the world, to testify to the truth. Everyone who is of the truth hears My voice" (John 18:37). Then, Pilate asked Jesus (18:38): "What is truth?" This question has been asked throughout history. All truth is God's truth, but our

subject has to do with the truth that leads to eternal life. Truth, in this sense, may be thought of in several ways.

First, one can think of truth as opposed to falsehood. Our salvation is based on a correct understanding of biblical truth about Christ. We must hear about Jesus, know what He has done for us, perceive our need for repentance and faith, and make our commitment to Christ. At the same time, we must reject false teachings that are against Christ. We must turn aside from all that would cause us to refuse the love and saving grace of our God.

Second, Jesus is the truth personified. All that we become in Christ is based on accepting Him as the truth. To know the truth, we simply have to look to Him. When we grow in the image of Christ, we are aligning ourselves with the truth. So our answer to the truth question is to focus our eyes on Jesus. Without Him, we will not have saving truth.

Third, in one sense of the word, truth is truth applied. It is something to be lived. Our knowledge of truth must go well beyond mere intellectual assent. The truth must have an impact on how we live. John makes this abundantly clear in 1 John 1:6–7:

> [6]If we say that we have fellowship with Him and *yet* walk in the darkness, we lie and do not practice the truth; [7]but if we walk in the Light as He Himself is in the Light, we have fellowship with one another, and the blood of Jesus His Son cleanses us from all sin.

All three of these views regarding "truth" are valid. Truth is content that is true as opposed to false; it must be centered in Christ; and it must be lived out in life. When these conditions prevail, we have truth that leads to eternal life. Obviously, faith in Christ is the crucial point.

4. *Attesting God is True*. In John 3:33, John writes, "He who has received His testimony has set his seal to *this*, that God is true." "He who has received His testimony" may refer specifically to John the Baptist, but every believer sets his seal, or attests, that God is true. The metaphor "seal" may have several meanings such as to keep something secret, to provide a mark of identification, to empower, and to attest. In this passage, "attestation" stands out. By accepting Christ's testimony through faith, the believers set their seal that God

is true and that Jesus speaks the message of God. They become witnesses of the truth of Christ's claims. This seal is best seen in the transformed lives of the believers. This transformation demonstrates in an individual's life who Christ is and what He has done.

Ultimately, it is God Himself who puts his seal upon Christ. John (6:27) states, "Do not work for the food which perishes, but for the food which endures to eternal life, which the Son of Man will give to you, for on Him the Father, God, has set His seal." According to some scholars, God sealed Jesus at His baptism in water; others point to the descent of the Spirit upon Christ. Still others refer to the miracles performed by Jesus. In my view, God sealed Jesus at different times and in different ways. The high point, however, was when God bestowed the Spirit upon Jesus.

5. *The Spirit of Truth.* Jesus called the Holy Spirit the Helper and the Spirit of Truth. Moreover, He identifies the Helper as the Spirit of Truth and refers to His coming. During His farewell discourse, Jesus speaks about the Helper four times (John 14:16; 14:26; 15:26; 16:7); and, in the same contexts, about the Spirit of Truth three times (John 14:17; 15:26; 16:13). In this way, Jesus emphasizes the connection between the Spirit and truth in His farewell discourse. When the Spirit of Truth comes, something new happens concerning truth and the communication of truth.

First, consider the meaning of the title "Spirit of Truth." The Greek language allows for a variety of interpretations of this title. These interpretations include: (1) the Spirit is the source of truth, (2) the Spirit communicates truth, (3) truth is characteristic of the Spirit, and (4) the Spirit applies truth. All of these interpretations are valid; but, "the Spirit who communicates truth" stands out (John 15:26; 16:13). In John 15:26, he states, "When the Helper comes, whom I will send to you from the Father, *that is* the Spirit of truth who proceeds from the Father, He will testify about Me."

Second, in 1 John 5:6–8, John says Jesus came by "water" and "blood." The meaning of the passage is much debated. As I understand it, the meaning is that the ministry of Christ is framed by His baptism in water and His death. Furthermore, it is the Spirit, the water, and the blood that testify on behalf of Jesus. Here the meaning is that the baptism of Jesus, the death of Christ, and the Spirit are all powerful witnesses.

Third, the mission of the Spirit as presented in John 14:26 is twofold. John states, "But the Helper, the Holy Spirit, whom the Father will send in My name, He will teach you all things, and bring to your remembrance all that I said to you." John stresses the comprehensiveness of what the Spirit will teach and emphasizes what Jesus already said. The Spirit will teach the disciples "all things." He will teach them all things that are necessary for their salvation and even more broadly all things that they need to know. The Spirit will help the disciples remember what Jesus had taught. He will call those things to their remembrance.

Fourth, in 1 John 4:6, John writes about the "spirit of truth and error." He is very concerned that the people of God know the truth, be taught the truth, and be protected from error. So there is a strong connection between Jesus, the Spirit, the truth, and the Word of God.

Fifth, when Jesus met with the woman of Samaria, she mentioned that the Samaritans worshiped at "this mountain" but that the Jews said Jerusalem was the place to worship. In response, Jesus said (John 4:23–24):

> [23]But an hour is coming, and now is, when the true worshipers will worship the Father in spirit and truth; for such people the Father seeks to be His worshipers. [24]God is spirit, and those who worship Him must worship in spirit and truth.

In other words, you can worship wherever you are. Our worship should be inspired by the Spirit, and it must be based on truth. Indeed, we must worship Christ, who is the truth. Our worship should continue by living the truth in all aspects of our lives.

Into All Truth

In John 16:13, Jesus declares, "But when He, the Spirit of truth, comes, He will guide you into all the truth; for He will not speak on His own initiative, but whatever He hears, He will speak; and He will disclose to you what is to come." Several points stand out in connection with this verse.

1. *Types of Truth.* One must consider both commentaries on truth already revealed as well as new truth. Indeed, the Spirit of Truth deals with everything that has to do with the truth. Several observations may be helpful.

First, based on textual evidence, scholars discuss whether Jesus said "into" or "in" all the truth. The preposition "into" emphasizes bringing into further knowledge, while the preposition "in" suggests leading you in the path already revealed. Actually, the Spirit guides one in the path of truth as well as leading into new vistas of truth. Another way of saying this is that the Spirit guides with regard to all aspects of truth.

With regard to commentary, the Spirit of Truth will elaborate on existing truth and illuminate believers' minds. The Spirit will interpret the words of Jesus. Many believers, for example, have experienced moments when the Spirit has enlightened them with the meaning of a passage of Scripture. These are great moments.

However, the Spirit of Truth is not limited to commentary. New truth will be advanced as well, but the new truth must not depart from the original revelation. We must keep in mind that, when Jesus spoke, the Word had not yet been written. The Holy Spirit would guide the authors. Any new truth advanced today does not have the same standing as the Word of God. The new truths will enrich and expand on the previously revealed truth. Very often, the new truths have to do with applying truth to believers' lives. Usually, the new truth can simply be classified as commentary on established truth.

One of the outstanding features of the early church was the guidance of the Spirit. For example, Paul and his team wanted to go to Bithynia, but as Luke says, "the Spirit of Jesus did not permit them" (Acts 16:7). The Spirit revealed to them that they should not go to Bithynia. Instead, they were called to Macedonia. Later, when writing to the Corinthians, Paul brings into focus the revelatory work of the Spirit through such gifts as prophecy, the word of knowledge, and the word of wisdom (1 Cor. 12:8–10). The Spirit is still manifesting these gifts today!

2. *Words of God.* The Holy Spirit speaks the words of God. Jesus says, "For He [the Holy Spirit] will not speak on His own initiative."

Like Christ (John 14:10), the Spirit will not speak on His own initiative but on what He hears. Jesus is referring to the source of the Spirit's teaching. He does not say that the Spirit will not speak "about" Himself. Obviously, the truth has to do with the Spirit as well as with the Father and the Son. Even so, the Spirit's ministry is to glorify Jesus. He speaks what He hears in order to exalt Christ.

Jesus emphasizes that the Spirit "shall take of Mine, and shall disclose *it* to you" (John 16:14). Jesus taught what he heard from the Father (John 8:26). The Spirit tells the disciples what He heard from Jesus (John 16:13). This, of course, does not preclude the fact that the Spirit hears from the Father as well.

3. *Things to Come*. The Spirit "will disclose to you what is to come." Various ideas are advanced concerning what Jesus meant by this statement. We can include all that is taught in the book of Revelation. Surely the things to come involved the work of the Spirit during the age of the church. Jesus is not explicit as to what He meant, so it is best not to be too dogmatic about it.

Conclusion

Eternal life! Truth! What dynamic, vital, and powerful truths! The Father, Son, and Holy Spirit all have a part in giving us eternal life. Christ is the truth! The Holy Spirit is the truth! Through faith in Christ and through the work of the Spirit, we can have eternal life. In addition, we can enjoy the fellowship of the saints who are growing in their knowledge of truth and in the image of Christ.

CHAPTER EIGHT

BAPTISM IN THE SPIRIT

In chapter four, I discussed many of the terms used concerning giving and receiving the Spirit. However, I have reserved my main comments on "baptism in the Spirit" until this chapter. Much of what I said in chapter four about the giving and receiving terms applies to baptism in the Spirit, but there are distinctions also.

The term "baptism" in the Spirit is not used in the Bible, but the term "baptize" in the Spirit is. The phrase "baptism in the Spirit" simply uses a noun in the place of the verb. The underlying reality is the same. It is both convenient and proper to use the term "baptism in the Spirit" when discussing this subject.

This term is commonly used by all branches of the church today to represent the presence and work of the Spirit. The common usage of the term does not, however, signify agreement on its meaning. Like the term "baptism" used in connection with water, this term is employed in a wide variety of ways.

Viewpoints

The term "baptism in the Spirit" has been applied both to the church and to individuals. When applied to the church, the baptism in the Spirit is considered to be a "once-and-for-all" event. Believers are encouraged to appropriate the benefit of that historic outpouring of the Spirit. Most writers, however, deal with the subject in terms of individuals.

With regard to individuals, the views about baptism in the Spirit are as varied as the theologies of the beginning of Christian life. Definitions of baptism in the Spirit are customized to fit the overall theology of various groups. Given the outpouring of the Spirit upon all branches of the church in recent decades, it is understandable that many theological understandings of baptism in the Spirit have developed.

At the outset, it should be recognized that definitions of baptism in the Spirit include non-sacramental and sacramental views. The views of these two groups are in many ways alike, except that they differ on how the baptism in the Spirit relates to the sacraments. Those who hold sacramental views may connect baptism in the Spirit with water baptism alone or to both baptism in water and confirmation. Those who do not hold sacramental views do not make a necessary connection between baptism in the Spirit and the church ordinances.

For my purposes, it will suffice to discuss the main non-sacramental approaches. Within these approaches, or views, there are many variations and nuances of thought. Therefore, the views presented here represent broad categories.

1. *Initiation*. One view is that baptism in the Spirit refers to the believer's initiation into the Christian life. The term has been applied to regeneration, indwelling of the Spirit, and entry into the body of Christ. Among those who hold to the initiation view, by far the majority view is that baptism in the Spirit refers to one's entry into the body of Christ or union with Christ. Many hold that baptism in the Spirit, thus conceived, is positional rather than experiential.

2. *Subsequent Experience*. Another view of baptism in the Spirit does not apply the term to initiation, but rather reserves it for a separate, distinct, and subsequent experience. Several viewpoints are held with regard to the purpose of this experience. Proponents may say that the purpose of baptism in the Spirit is for sanctification, assurance of salvation, empowerment for service, the outward flow of love from believers' lives, or other reasons. Emphasis is placed on baptism in the Spirit being an experience that can be perceived, and one knows when it happens. Many advocates of this view hold that the believer may have additional crisis experiences with the Spirit, not just a second experience.

3. *"Both–And" Approach*. Some expositors hold to the view that baptism in the Spirit can refer *both* to being baptized into the body of Christ *and* to the separate experience of being empowered for various purposes. This is a "both–and" approach that avoids choosing between the first two approaches. With regard to the purpose of the baptism in the Spirit, proponents of this view may emphasize purity,

power for witness, or both. Obviously, under this view, the metaphor of baptism in the Spirit is used in more than one way.

4. *Initiation Elements*. Other scholars hold that Spirit-baptism belongs with the set of elements that make up Christian initiation. Another element is baptism in water. Obviously, those who hold this view still face issues such as the purpose of the baptism in the Spirit, whether or not it is necessary in Christian initiation, and exactly when it occurs in relationship to other elements. The proponents of this view sometimes seek to avoid the thought that the body of Christ is made up of those who have been baptized in the Spirit and those who have not. Therefore, they tie baptism in the Spirit to the initiation of Christian life.

5. *Dimension of the Spirit*. Some writers, especially in the Charismatic Movement, view baptism in the Spirit as a dimension of the Spirit's presence and work. Usually, this dimension is considered to be experiential. The emphasis may be upon a living faith, the Spirit of prophecy, or simply all aspects of Christian life made alive. Although baptism in the Spirit is closely tied to Christian initiation, the ongoing aspect of the Spirit's work is recognized. In a sense, this is a variation of the fourth approach above.

6. *Inclusive*. An inclusive view is that baptism in the Spirit refers to all of the Spirit's work in the lives of the believers. The work of the Spirit includes regeneration, justification, sanctification, sealing, empowerment for witness and service, the outpouring of love, and other elements. Sometimes, the ongoing work of the Spirit is emphasized, but a crisis experience with the Spirit may be included as well.

The major Pentecostal communities hold a view of baptism in the Spirit that fits mainly in the second category listed above. Some features of their view may be drawn from other categories as well. Moreover, the doctrinal statements of these communities, as far as I know, do not preclude the use of the term in other ways. Along with most of the views, Pentecostals stress the ongoing and vital relationship of the believer with the Spirit. The believer should continually be filled with the Spirit.

Scriptural Data

All four Gospels mention the baptism in the Spirit. However, the experiences that are said to be baptisms in the Spirit are described in the book of Acts. As Luke describes these experiences, they are highly experiential. Another possible reference is by Paul in his first letter to the Corinthians. We will review what Luke says as well as the comments of the other authors. Out of all the evidence will emerge the picture that we need to see.

1. *John the Baptist.* It was John the Baptist who originally used the term "baptized" or "baptizes" in the Holy Spirit. His usage of this term is cited by all four of the Gospel writers (Matt. 3:11; Mark 1:8; Luke 3:16; John 1:33). Matthew and Luke add "and fire," while Mark and John write simply "Holy Spirit."

According to Matthew, Mark, and Luke, John the Baptist said that Jesus "will baptize" you in the Holy Spirit. They use the future tense. However, the author John cites John the Baptist as saying "baptizes," which is a present tense. Although Matthew, Mark, and Luke employ the future tense, they do not explicitly say when the future begins. When Johns uses the present tense, it can refer rhetorically to the future, but clearly its primary reference is to something currently happening. Grammatically, it is possible to hold that Jesus baptized in the Spirit in some way before His glorification but in a greater sense later.

As John the Baptist used the term, the baptism in the Spirit will result in the separation of the wheat and the chaff (Luke 3:17). He may have had in mind the inner cleansing of the believer as well. When the apostle John cited John the Baptist (John 1:33), he may have implied that the Spirit would enable the disciples to make Christ known to the world. It may be, also, that John thought the term could be applied to all the work of the Spirit in the life of the believer.

We should not limit what John understood by the phrase "in Holy Spirit and fire." This phrase, I believe, refers to the Holy Spirit in action. The Holy Spirit is engaged in many activities. Like most metaphors, "baptism" and "fire" are flexible and can mean different things. Both John and Jesus preached salvation and judgment. The Holy Spirit, with fire-like action, can administer both redemption and judgment (Luke 3:16–17). When Christ returns, the ultimate consummation of the judgment will take place. The fulfillment of John the Baptist's statement is not limited to one time and place.

2. *Jesus*. We know that Jesus applied the phrase "baptized in the Spirit" to the outpouring of the Spirit at Pentecost (Acts 1:4–5). The predominant purpose (Acts 1:8) of that outpouring was to empower the disciples to witness worldwide. This worldwide witness would confront men with the claims of Christ and result ultimately in the separation of the wheat and the chaff. This would be in harmony with the original statement of John the Baptist.

3. *Peter*. According to Peter, the believers at Caesarea were baptized in the Spirit (Acts 11:16). What the believers experienced was the baptism in the Spirit that John the Baptist spoke about. Peter said their experience was "the same gift" that the disciples received at Pentecost (Acts 11:15–17; 15:8). Thus, the term "baptism in the Spirit" describes the experiences of the disciples at both Pentecost and Caesarea.

4. *Paul*. In 1 Corinthians 12:13, Paul says, "For by [*en*] one Spirit we were all baptized into [*eis*] one body, whether Jews or Greeks, whether slaves or free, and we were all made to drink of one Spirit." The Greek preposition *en* can be translated "in," "by" or "with." The preposition *eis* can mean "into," "unto," or "with reference to." This is the only time that Paul uses the phrase "baptized *en* the Spirit."

The first clause of this verse is translated by many scholars as "*by* the Spirit *into* one body." I would agree that this is the primary meaning, but the Greek prepositions allow for a wide variety of interpretations. For example, it could mean "*in* the Spirit *unto* one body." Whether you translate *en* as "in" or "by," this clause could refer not only to the formation of the body Christ but also to its functioning. Neither the grammar nor the context (cp. 1 Cor. 12:3, 9) is absolutely decisive for any interpretation. This may be an instance of Paul using a term more comprehensively than Luke.

It is interesting that, in 1 Corinthians 10:2, a similar grammatical construction is used. Paul wrote, "and all were baptized *into* [*eis*] Moses *in* [*en*] the cloud and in the sea." When the Israelites crossed the Red Sea, they became a part of the Moses movement. One could say that they were baptized either *by* or *in* the cloud and the sea respectively *into* Moses or *unto* Moses. The end result is about the same, but *by* the cloud and the sea is probably preferable.

5. *Filled and Baptized.* Many people use the terms "baptize" and "filled" with the Spirit interchangeably. They rightly observe, for example, that the book of Acts uses both terms to describe the experience of the disciples at Pentecost. However, terms may be used interchangeably in some cases without being totally synonymous. It is better to say that these terms overlap in meaning. As we indicated in chapter four, the terms for giving and receiving the Spirit sometimes overlap, but each term may have its own distinctive meaning as well.

Some expositors distinguish between baptism in the Spirit and being filled with the Spirit. They hold that baptism in the Spirit is the initial experience of being filled, but one may be filled many times. However, we do not need to limit the term "baptism in the Spirit" to the initial filling. We might say that we were baptized in the Spirit, are being baptized in the Spirit, and will be baptized in the Spirit. The baptism in the Spirit may be more than a one-time experience.

6. *Flexible Metaphor.* As discussed in chapter four, we use terms such as "promise," "give," "receive," "filled," "poured out," and "anointed" in flexible ways. Normally, Paul uses such terms more broadly than Luke. Some scholars maintain that the metaphor "baptized in the Spirit" is flexible enough to cover both our union with the body of Christ and our empowerment for witness. Similarly, some hold that this metaphor can refer to both the position and the experience of being baptized in the Spirit. The potential of baptism in the Spirit is actualized in the lives of believers.

The Baptism Metaphor

What does the metaphor of baptism contribute to one's understanding of the baptism in the Spirit as presented in the book of Acts? Following is a list of some of the characteristics of water baptism. As each characteristic is listed, notice how baptism in the Spirit compares. With regard to the Spirit, the two cases that are called baptisms in the Spirit—Pentecost and Caesarea—will be considered.

1. *Historical Event.* Baptism is an observable event. It is something that one can see and report. It does not just quietly happen. Its very purpose demands a historical happening. It involves a baptizer, the one baptized, usually witnesses, and water.

Both at Pentecost and at Caesarea, something notable and observable happened. The baptizer is Jesus, the believer is baptized, the element is the Spirit, and there were witnesses. At Pentecost, some of the audience mocked, saying, "They are full of sweet wine" (Acts 2:13). It was clear to Peter and others at Caesarea that the Spirit had been poured out on the Gentiles. The outpouring of the Spirit upon them was sufficient evidence for Peter to baptize them in water.

Those who maintain that baptism in the Spirit is only a part of the non-experiential work of the Spirit at salvation tend to lose this element of metaphorical significance. The metaphor is particularly suited to baptism in the Spirit as experiential empowerment. It is the kind of experience that one can frequently recall in testimony to others.

2. *Witness.* Water baptism is a time of witness. The event gives witness to the saving grace of Christ. Just how it is related to salvation is debated, but the fact that baptism provides a witness is not. The purpose of the baptism is to demonstrate and lay claim to the fact that the one baptized is a child of God. The one who is baptized testifies to the saving grace of God. In many baptismal ceremonies, the one baptized verbally acknowledges his commitment to Christ.

The baptism in the Spirit was a moment of witness. At Pentecost, the audience heard the disciples speaking in tongues (Acts 2:4). The audience said, "We hear them in our *own* tongues speaking of the mighty deeds of God" (Acts 2:11). At Caesarea, the Gentiles were "speaking in tongues and exalting God" (Acts 10:46). The disciples were powerfully telling others about God. Then, at Ephesus, the disciples "*began* speaking with tongues and prophesying." This, too, was a witness to those present. When the Spirit was outpoured at Samaria, Simon "saw" that the disciples were receiving the Holy Spirit (Acts 8:18). Luke does not say what he saw, but the experience definitely bore witness.

3. *Attestation*. Baptism in water carries with it the attestation of the church. When the believer is baptized, he not only testifies to his salvation, but the church also recognizes him as a believer. Thus, the ceremony has value to the redeemed individual and to the body of Christ.

When the Spirit came upon the Gentiles at Caesarea, Peter knew that God had cleansed their hearts by faith. The very presence of the Spirit attested to their salvation. As a result, Peter was prepared to baptize them in water. Without this attestation, Peter might have hesitated to baptize the Gentiles. This was a major breakthrough in the church's expansion.

4. *Initiation*. Water baptism has an initiatory character. Normally, it happens at the beginning of Christian life and is not repeated. When people are baptized, they publicly enter the Christian life, and one baptism suffices. When Christians are being persecuted, baptism is a "point of no return" kind of event.

Many believe that the initiatory character of the term "baptism in water" applies to baptism in the Spirit. Some writers hold that baptism in the Spirit is only the initial experience of the believer. Those who hold this view may use the term "filled with the Spirit" with regard to additional experiences. However, it is not necessary to limit the metaphor of baptism to an initial experience. In my view, the "one-time event" characteristic of water baptism does not necessarily apply.

5. *Immersion*. In my understanding, baptism in water was an immersion in water. I acknowledge, of course, that others sprinkle with water instead of immersing. The figure of immersion is especially powerful with respect to Spirit baptism. The real essence of being baptized in the Spirit is to be immersed in the Spirit's presence. The word "immersion" is itself a metaphor having to do with the impact of the Spirit on our lives.

Pentecostal Baptism

The views of Pentecostals on the baptism in the Spirit are derived mainly from Luke's usage of this metaphor and the experience of the disciples at Pentecost and Caesarea. Unless otherwise stated, this is what Pentecostals normally mean by baptism in the Holy Spirit. Luke uses "baptized in the Spirit" three times (Luke 3:16; Acts 1:4–5; 11:16). In these verses, he respectively cites John the Baptist, Jesus, and Peter. With regard to interpreting this experience, Luke stresses the comments made by Jesus and Peter. So, to a large extent, our Pentecostal views are based on their comments. These passages are the primary basis for the following discussion.

1. *Purposes.* The pouring forth of the Spirit on the Day of Pentecost and at Caesarea made known to us the central purposes of the baptism in the Spirit. On both occasions, the disciples had an observable experience. At Pentecost, the disciples had a crisis experience (Acts 2:4–11) that resulted in empowered witness through speaking in tongues and exalting the mighty deeds of God. At the house of Cornelius, the Spirit was outpoured upon the Gentiles. This vital experience demonstrated that God had accepted the faith of the Gentiles. God attested that the Gentiles and their faith were accepted. So attestation is an additional purpose that is supported by Scripture (Acts 10:44-48). Although other purposes often are attributed to baptism in the Spirit, these two results stand out in the history written by Luke.

2. *Subsequence.* As Pentecostals, we hold that the baptism in the Spirit, as experienced at Pentecost, is subsequent to regeneration. In my view, a very strong case for subsequence can be made on the ground that there is an objective aspect of salvation to which all experience is subsequent. Our initial objective reception of the Spirit is followed by ongoing and repeated reception, including the baptism in the Holy Spirit. The experiential baptism in the Spirit may occur at about the same time as other experiential aspects of salvation (Acts 10:44–48).

3. *Speaking in Tongues.* Luke records three instances when the disciples spoke in tongues or other languages. These occurred in Jerusalem on the Day of Pentecost, later at the house of Cornelius in Caesarea, and again at Ephesus. At Jerusalem and Caesarea, Luke says the disciples were baptized in the Spirit. When the Holy Spirit "came on" the disciples at Ephesus (Acts 19:6), they spoke in tongues and prophesied. In this case, Luke does not use the term "baptized in the Spirit." It was an instance of receiving the Spirit (Acts 19:2).

When the believers at Pentecost and Caesarea were baptized in the Spirit, they spoke in tongues. Many Pentecostals say that speaking in tongues is not the baptism in the Spirit, but rather the evidence of the baptism. Others regard speaking in tongues as an integral part of the experience. When this evidence is required, there is little difference between these views. At Pentecost and Caesarea, speaking in tongues clearly was a part of the event. One can say that speaking in tongues was a way in which the baptized believers witnessed.

At Pentecost (Acts 2:4, 6, 11), the disciples spoke in languages that they had not learned but that the people present understood. As far as we know, at Caesarea (Acts 10:46) and Ephesus (Acts 19:6), the people present did not understand the words that were spoken in tongues. With regard to speaking in tongues as evidence of the baptism in the Spirit, the main point is that the tongues, or other languages, are unknown to the speakers. When Peter heard the Gentiles speaking in tongues and exalting God at Caesarea (Acts 10:46–47, 15:8), he regarded the gift of the Spirit there as the same gift the disciples received at Pentecost.

4. *Pattern.* As Pentecostals, we hold that believers today are eligible to be baptized in the Spirit in a manner analogous to what the disciples experienced in Jerusalem on the Day of Pentecost. Not every aspect of what happened on the Day of Pentecost was repeated. However, the apostle Peter regarded the experience of the Gentiles at Caesarea as analogous. The view that the experience of the disciples at Pentecost provides a pattern for believers today is at the heart of Pentecost. As Pentecostals, we base this view in part on inductive reasoning.

Moreover, the inductive approach applies to both the observable experience and the speaking in tongues. Some expositors use inductive arguments to support the crisis experience but reject similar arguments for speaking in tongues. Pentecostals usually apply the inductive reasoning to both.

Several cases are included by Pentecostals in this inductive examination. At Pentecost, the disciples had an observable experience that the disciples made evident by speaking in tongues. The experiences of the disciples at Caesarea and Ephesus were similar. At Samaria (Acts 8:18), Simon "saw" that the Spirit was given through the laying on of hands. Luke does not say what he saw, but some scholars think the Samaritans spoke in tongues. With regard to Saul (Paul), Ananias was sent to him so that he might be "filled" with the Spirit (Acts 9:17). Luke does not record what happened. We do know that speaking in tongues was a part of Paul's spiritual experience.

The inductive evidence is valuable, but Peter gives us a propositional statement in Acts 2:38–39 that is even more helpful. This statement supports Pentecost as a pattern. According to Luke, "Peter *said* to them, 'Repent and each of you be baptized in the name of Jesus Christ for the forgiveness of your sins; and you will receive the gift of the Holy Spirit. For the promise is for you and your children and for all who are far off, as many as the Lord our God will call to Himself.'"

What did Peter mean by "the gift of the Holy Spirit?" Surely, he had in mind, as an expected result, at least what had just happened on the Day of Pentecost. The disciples enjoyed a crisis experience accompanied by speaking in tongues. Such an experience was foreseen by Peter as being for everyone who believes in Christ. However, the phrase "gift of the Spirit" no doubt has broader implications as well. Certainly the word "promise" is more broadly used in the New Testament. As I see it, this passage can refer also to the initial indwelling of the Spirit.

5. *Eligibility*. All believers are commanded to be baptized in water. This is the common understanding of all branches of the church. The New Testament, throughout, assumes that all who unite with Christ are to be baptized. Depending on a church's theology, even the children of believers are either "dedicated" or "baptized."

Baptism in the Spirit, like baptism in water, is for all believers. No matter what definition of baptism in the Spirit is upheld, the proponents virtually all agree that this baptism is for all. However, views diverge with regard to how the baptism occurs. Those who regard baptism in the Spirit as entry into the body of Christ say it occurs right away in response to saving faith. For those who see baptism in the Spirit as empowerment, all believers are eligible to receive this gift.

6. *Seek the Baptism.* We should present the baptism in the Spirit, according to Acts 2:4 and 10:46, as an experience to be desired for the purposes stated above. The Pentecostal model is powerful and rich in value. It is an event that happens in history which we can recall throughout our lives. We certainly are in order to encourage all believers to be in harmony with this pattern. Our people should "ardently expect" and "earnestly seek" the baptism in the Spirit.

7. *Role of Faith.* We should emphasize the role of faith. When a person believes in Christ, he or she automatically receives a twofold gift—union with Christ and reception of the Spirit. However, as with all promises, the promise of the Spirit baptism must be appropriated through faith. We do not accept Christ and then live without the ongoing exercise of faith. So, the believer must come in humility and faith to Jesus, the baptizer, to be baptized in the Spirit.

Special Issues

1. *Baptism in Water.* Several key passages are cited by Pentecostals with regard to the baptism in the Spirit. All of these instances are closely connected in time to water baptism. The instances include Pentecost (Acts 2:38–39), Samaria (Acts 8:12–13), Damascus (Acts 9:18), Caesarea (Acts 10:48), and Ephesus (Acts 19:5). Baptism in the Spirit and baptism in water are separate experiences, but they often occurred near the beginning of Christian life. Let it be this way with new believers today!

2. *Dimensions.* What impact does the baptism in the Spirit have on the various dimensions of the Spirit? Any experience with the Holy Spirit can have an impact on all aspects of our Christian lives. However, it would seem appropriate that the dimensions Luke describes in the book of Acts would especially be included. We have identified those dimensions in chapter six. They mainly have to do with carrying out the mission of witnessing to the entire world.

We should neither claim too much nor too little for the experience, but it is for us as believers. The impact of the baptism in the Spirit can mean different things to different people. There is a great deal of individuality in our experience. Our testimonies as to what the experience means to us vary by quite a bit. It is safe to say that this experience can impact any and even all of our experience with the Lord in positive ways. The baptism in the Spirit fits fully and harmoniously into all of our Christian lives. The Holy Spirit's empowerment to witness should be a common denominator. All baptized believers should be active in exalting the name of Christ.

3. *Gateway*. The baptism in the Spirit, accompanied by speaking in tongues, very often opens the door to the expression of spiritual gifts and a closer relationship with the Spirit. However, it is not a required gateway to experiencing the Spirit in His various dimensions, including the exercise of spiritual gifts. The baptism in the Spirit enhances our exercise of spiritual gifts and has a positive impact on us in all dimensions of the Spirit. However, we cannot say that believers who have not been baptized in the Spirit cannot experience the Spirit in His many dimensions. Ultimately, our actual experience with the Spirit is more important than what we call it.

We have to be cautious when we try to define what others have not experienced. With regard to all believers, those who have spoken in tongues and those who have not, there are many dimensions to our relationship with the Spirit. We must continue to grow with regard to all of these dimensions. We have oceans to swim in with regard to the fruit of the Spirit, the gifts of the Spirit, and other dimensions of the Spirit. None can boast, and all must be responsible for continued growth.

4. *Already–Not Yet*. We should acknowledge that many believers who have not spoken in tongues may already have very rich experience with the Holy Spirit. Even so, we may still urge them to "earnestly seek" the baptism in the Holy Spirit according to Acts 2:4. This is an experience that they have "not yet" received. By genuinely speaking in tongues, they will be assured that they have been baptized in the Spirit after the model at Pentecost. We believe there is great value in having a crisis experience with the Spirit. This does not minimize the value of other types of experience.

Conclusion

The term "baptism" is a metaphor. As such, it is flexible and can signify various meanings. The church has employed this term to apply to baptism in water and to baptism in the Spirit. In both cases, the church historically has had great debates over the precise meanings of the terms. With regard to baptism in the Spirit, the meanings assigned are as varied as the doctrinal views of different branches of the church about the initiation of Christian life. Even so, many believers have found common ground with others through their relationship with the Spirit and their experience of His presence and works.

When Pentecostals use the term "baptism in the Spirit," they mainly refer to the outpouring of the Spirit on the Day of Pentecost and at Caesarea. However, this does not preclude the use of the baptism metaphor in other ways and with various meanings. The baptism in the Spirit at Jerusalem and Caesarea was for empowered witness and attestation of the believers. As believers, we all are eligible for this baptism in the Spirit. Through faith in Christ, the baptizer, let us be baptized in the Spirit.

CHAPTER NINE

FRUIT AND GIFTS

The apostle Paul was comprehensive in his treatment of the dimensions of the Spirit. As a convenience, I have organized the Pauline data about the Spirit under the headings of life, maturity, ministry, and worship. One of the aspects of the maturity dimension that Paul emphasizes is the fruit of the Spirit. With regard to the ministry dimension, he stresses the gifts of the Spirit.

As Paul makes clear, both the fruit of the Spirit and the gifts of the Spirit are vitally important to spiritual life. We must have both fruit and gifts. Those who would exercise gifts without fruit will find that their lives are shallow and ultimately without significant spiritual blessing. Those who would want fruit without gifts do not employ all of the ministry tools that the Spirit provides. They will not fulfill God's call for them to minister effectively to others. What we need is fruit and gifts together.

Walk and Fruit

A major passage with regard to the believer's walk and the fruit of the Spirit is given by the apostle Paul in Galatians 5:16–26. Paul exhorts the believer to walk in the Spirit and to manifest the fruit of the Spirit. There is a struggle between the flesh and the Spirit. The Spirit helps the believer overcome in this battle. With the help of the Holy Spirit, the believer develops ethically. This spiritual development is the experiential actualization of positional sanctification.

The apostle Paul, in his epistle to the Galatians, answers the Judaizers who maintained the believers could not become good Christians without adhering to certain Jewish practices. As Paul answers them, he deals with subjects such as the flesh, the Law, the Holy Spirit, and the fruit of the Spirit. He shows how all these factors are related to each other and the ethical life of the believer.

In Paul's theology, we live in this present age, between the past and the future ages. Christ has defeated Satan through His death and resurrection (John 16:11; Col. 2:15). The consummation of that victory will come in the future. Meanwhile, Satan, who is the "god of this age" (2 Cor. 4:4 NIV) is still at work, blinding the eyes of the unbelieving. That is why we still have a battle with the forces of evil. Our future victory is certain. Paul says, "The God of peace will soon crush Satan under your feet" (Rom. 16:20). Ultimately, Satan will be cast into the lake of fire (Rev. 20:10).

As Paul ministers to Jewish believers, the Law is a very important topic. In Galatians 3:1–5, Paul makes it clear that the Christians had received the Spirit through faith and not by the works of the Law. Moreover, he declares (Gal. 5:14) that the whole Law is fulfilled in one word which is love. It is through the Spirit that the moral Law is fulfilled. We are now living under the new covenant, which is a covenant of the Spirit (2 Cor. 3:6), not of the letter. The letter kills, but the Spirit gives life.

Now we will turn to Galatians 5:16–26. This is Paul's classic passage on walking by the Spirit and manifesting the fruit of the Spirit. Everyone who desires to fully follow Christ is challenged throughout his life by this great passage.

1. *Verse 16*. Paul says, "Walk by [*en*] the Spirit, and you will not carry out the desire of the flesh." Here, Paul uses the preposition *en*. It makes little difference whether we translate this preposition as *by* or *in*. We walk in the sphere of the Spirit, and He enables us to so walk. Actually, the meanings overlap. As the Spirit enables us, He is present within us. With regard to the believer, the Spirit is present within as He works.

The word "flesh" in Scripture can have several meanings. The meaning in this verse is that the Galatians were giving in to their sinful tendencies. As a result, there was a lot of strife in the community (Gal. 5:15). A sign that the Galatians were not fully walking by the Spirit was that they were biting and devouring one another. If they would walk by the Spirit, they would overcome this tendency. As we walk by and in the Spirit, we are assured of ethical victory.

2. *Verse 17*. Paul writes about the conflict between the flesh and the Spirit. He says, "The flesh sets its desire against the Spirit, and the Spirit against the flesh; for these are in opposition to one another,

so that you may not do the things that you please." Two key considerations stand out.

First, Paul personifies "flesh" as he places it in opposition to "Spirit." The "flesh" has sinful desires, but the Spirit has only holy desires. The phrase "sets its desire" simply means "to long for." Thus, it can be used with both the flesh and the Spirit; the flesh longs for evil things, while the Spirit longs for holy things. The flesh and the Spirit do battle with each other. As long as we live in this present age, this battle will continue.

Second, the last clause of this verse says, "so that you may not do the things that you please." Paul is writing to the believers at Galatia, so we should assume that the pronoun "you" refers to Christians. Just how this verse applies to Christians is subject to various interpretations. Without attempting to comment on all of them, I will present two main lines of thought.

One, some commentators favor a view that could read like this: "so that you, under the influence of the flesh, may not do the *good* things that you desire to do even though you have the Spirit within." In other words, the flesh blocks you as you attempt to follow the Spirit's leading. You cannot do the ethical things you want to do. Assuming this is what Paul meant, we as believers would appear to be unable to overcome the flesh. This view seems to be in conflict with the victory described in verse 16. It is true that the battle between flesh and Spirit continues throughout our lives, but we are not defeated. We may lose a battle, but we will not lose the war.

Two, another line of thought might read like this: "so that you, under the influence of the Spirit, may not do the things that you, under the influence of the flesh, desire to do." In other words, the Spirit persuasively guides the life of the Christian and overcomes the flesh. You may not do what the flesh wants because of the Spirit's presence within. This approach is in full harmony with verse 16. However, we know that the victory is not yet absolute. The believer is not sinless, but he does not practice sin. Ultimately, the victory of Christ will be fully consummated in the life of each believer.

3. *Verse 18*. Paul states, "If you are led by the Spirit, you are not under the Law." Here, Paul moves from the contrast between flesh and

the Spirit to a contrast between the Spirit and the Law. The Law provides a standard, but it does not enable you to live up to the standard. The Spirit enables us to overcome the flesh. Given this, we do not live under the Law because we live up to God's standard without it. The Law, in its moral aspects, is fulfilled when people live by the Spirit.

When Paul says "you are led" (*agesthe*), he uses the present tense. This can have the force of being continually led. We can interpret this to mean "as long as you are being led by the Spirit," you are not under the Law. When we are led by the Spirit, we do not need the Law to govern our ethical actions. With regard to "law," many think that law in general is intended. Certainly the principle applies to all law. However, Paul specifically has in mind the Law of Moses.

4. *Verses 19–21.* Paul lists the deeds of the flesh and makes a strong statement about the eternal impact of the deeds on the lives of the Galatians. They will not inherit the kingdom of God. This is not a popular message today. Many people would prefer to think of God as being eternally tolerant of their sins.

> [19]Now the deeds of the flesh are evident, which are: immorality, impurity, sensuality, [20]idolatry, sorcery, enmities, strife, jealousy, outbursts of anger, disputes, dissensions, factions, [21]envying, drunkenness, carousing, and things like these, of which I forewarn you, just as I have forewarned you, that those who practice such things will not inherit the kingdom of God.

5. *Verses 22–23.* Paul now mentions the fruit of the Spirit. New Testament believers are to be exemplified by these fruit. When we manifest the fruit of the Spirit, the whole body of Christ is blessed. Obviously, there are differences in the body of Christ with regard to the fruit of the Spirit. Some people are strong in one fruit, while others are known for different fruit. Moreover, each believer may be more mature in connection with one fruit than he is with others. We know, however, that all believers should grow with regard to all of the fruit. Paul says:

> [22]But the fruit of the Spirit is love, joy, peace, patience, kindness, goodness, faithfulness, [23]gentleness, self-control; against such things there is no law.

As disciples, we should be characterized by these fruit as well as other fruit not listed here. The fruit are the fruit of the Spirit. As we walk with Christ, the Spirit grows the fruit in our lives. The Law stands against the deeds of the flesh, but there is no law against the fruit of the Spirit. No one, under any law, seeks to prohibit the manifestation of these characteristics. These characteristics make us like Christ. When we believe in Christ as Savior, we believe that the Spirit will be at work in us, developing us in the image of our Lord. Paul says, "But we all, with unveiled face, beholding as in a mirror the glory of the Lord, are being transformed into the same image from glory to glory, just as from the Lord, the Spirit" (2 Cor. 3:18).

6. *Verses 24–26.* In verse 24, those who belong to Christ have crucified the flesh with its passions and desires. Paul writes (v. 25), "If we live [*zōmen*] by the Spirit, let us also walk [*stoichōmen*] by the Spirit." The NEB translates it as, "If the Spirit is the source of our life, let the Spirit also direct our course." The Spirit quickened believers, made them new, and continually gives them life. They should, therefore, act accordingly. The believers' daily steps should be controlled by the Spirit. Both verbs in this verse are in the present tense. Given this, Christians continue to live and to walk by means of the Spirit. In verse 26, Paul exhorts us, "Let us not become boastful, challenging one another, envying one another."

Ministry and Spiritual Gifts

In Paul's thought, "the ministry" is the ministry of the Spirit. He devotes a full chapter to this concept (2 Cor. 3). His thinking focuses on the relationship of the ministry of the Spirit to the new covenant. The crux of the new covenant is the transformed inner life. Thus, the ministry of the Spirit has to do with the realization of righteousness in men. A major goal is to help men develop in the maturity dimension.

Under the old covenant, the empowerment of the Spirit was very evident. Clearly, the new covenant assimilates and includes all of the promises of the old with regard to empowered ministry. The ministry of the Spirit is powerful. By word and deed, in the power of the Spirit, the Spirit-led minister does great things. All of this leads one to the exercise of the gifts of the Spirit, which are mainly ways to minister for the Lord. The gifts of the Spirit are ways to serve in the kingdom of God. Several general points about spiritual gifts in ministry are as follows:

1. *Key Passages.* The major passages where Paul deals with spiritual gifts are found in Romans 12:6–8, 1 Corinthians 12–14, and Ephesians 4:7–13. These lists do not exhaust all possibilities, but they do indicate that there are many gifts. To these, one could add Romans 1:11; 1 Corinthians 1:7; 13:1–3, 8; 1 Timothy 4:13–14; and 2 Timothy 1:6–7.

2. *The Triune Giver.* In Pauline thinking, God (Rom. 12:3), Christ (Eph. 4:7, 11), and the Spirit (1 Cor. 12:11) are the direct givers of gifts. In 2 Timothy 1:6, Timothy's gift is specifically called the "gift of God." Because we serve the Triune God, it should not be surprising that the bestowal of gifts is attributed to all three Persons. Furthermore, we should not try to draw too many distinctions based on who is the named giver.

3. *Purposes.* The gifts of the Spirit are many, but a well-known list of nine is found in 1 Corinthians 12:7–11. This passage makes known that these gifts are given for the common good (verse 7) and that the Spirit distributes (v. 11) them according to His will. These same purposes apply to the gifts listed in other passages (Rom. 12:3–8; Eph. 4:11–12). In 1 Corinthians 12:7–11, Paul writes:

> [7]But to each one is given the manifestation of the Spirit for the common good. [8]For to one is given the word of wisdom through the Spirit, and to another the word of knowledge according to the same Spirit; [9]to another faith by the same Spirit, and to another gifts of healing by the one Spirit, [10]and to another the effecting of miracles, and to another prophecy, and to another the distinguishing of spirits, to another *various* kinds of tongues, and to another the interpretation of tongues. [11]But one and the same Spirit works all these things, distributing to each one individually just as He wills.

4. *Ministries.* Spiritual gifts include both ministerial positions and ministries (Eph. 4:11; 1 Cor. 12:28–30; Rom. 12:6–8) that various people held and expressed respectively in the early church. All of these positions and ministries should be present in the church today with the exception of apostles in the narrow sense of the term. Narrowly speaking, the term "apostles" refers only to the apostles in the early church. When the term is used in a broad sense, it refers to

anyone "sent on a mission." Similarly, the term "prophet" is often reserved in common usage for people who are being used of God in outstanding ways. However, in a broader way, the Spirit is poured out Acts upon all mankind and all can prophesy (Acts 2:17–18; 1 Cor. 14:31). No one today, of course, has the ministry of composing Scriptures as did some of the apostles and prophets of the past.

5. *Luke's Writings*. Luke mentions the "gift" of the Spirit, but he does not mention "gifts" of the Spirit. We often identify actions in Luke and Acts as gifts, but Luke does not. Some writers categorize various divine works in Acts under one or more of the gifts. For example, some scholars say that Peter's knowledge of Ananias lying came as a "word of knowledge." This may be, but it is not a point that Luke makes. Like Luke, John does not speak about the "gifts" of the Spirit. However, the writer of Hebrews does mention gifts or distributions of the Spirit. He says, "God also testifying with them, both by signs and wonders and by various miracles and by gifts [*merismois,* distributions] of the Holy Spirit according to His own will" (2:4).

Spiritual Gifts Described

As we study the gifts of the Spirit, it is important to have a complete picture of all of the gifts. We often speak of the nine gifts, but as indicated above, there are many more. Also, we must take into account how Paul described the gifts. So, we will turn now to this subject.

1. *Terms*. Three different Greek terms are used by Paul to designate spiritual gifts: (1) *pneumatikōn*, (2) *charismata*, and (3) *domata*. These terms illustrate the richness and variety of his language about the Spirit.
- 1 Corinthians 12:1. Paul uses the word Greek word *pneumatikōn* for spiritual gifts. Here, this substantive adjective may be neuter, meaning "spiritual gifts," or masculine, meaning "spiritual persons." It is not necessary to decide between persons and gifts, because spiritual persons have spiritual gifts.
- Romans 1:11. Paul writes to the Romans, expressing this wish: "For I long to see you in order that I may impart some

spiritual gift (*pneumatikōn*) to you, that you may be established." Clearly, in this context, Paul refers to a spiritual gift, not a spiritual person.

- Galatians 6:1. Here, Paul uses the word *pneumatikoi* in the context of spiritual maturity. Therefore, we have this translation: "you who are spiritual." This demonstrates that the word is not limited to a spiritual gift. In a sense, a spiritual man is a spiritual gift as well.
- 1 Corinthians 14:1. Here, Paul says, "If anyone thinks he is a prophet or spiritual (*pneumatikos*), let him recognize that the things which I write to you are the Lord's commandment." In this case, the adjective is masculine and refers to a spiritual man.
- Romans 12:6. Paul says, "we have gifts (*charismata*) that differ according to the grace (*charin*) given to us." The Greek word *charis* means "grace" and is used by Paul concerning all that God freely does for us.
- 1 Corinthians 12:4, 31. In 1 Corinthians 12:4, Paul says, "Now there are varieties of gifts (*charismatōn*), but the same Spirit." Paul speaks in 1 Corinthians 12:31 about the "greater gifts" (*ta charismata ta meizona*). He lists several gifts in 1 Corinthians 12:28–30, including some that are not in verses 8–10.
- Ephesians 4:8. In this verse, Paul cites Psalm 68:18 in a reference to the Messiah. With regard to Christ, he says: "And He gave gifts (*domata*) to men." According to Ephesians 4:11, the gifts included apostles, prophets, evangelists, and pastors and teachers or pastors-teachers.

2. *Threefold Description.* In 1 Corinthians 12:4–6, Paul gives a threefold description of spiritual gifts. While doing this, he reveals that all three Persons of the Godhead are involved in the giving and operation of the various gifts. Also, he points out that these gifts are for ministry; they are ways to serve in the church.

[4]Now there are varieties of gifts, but the same Spirit. [5]And there are varieties of ministries, and the same Lord. [6]There are varieties of effects, but the same God who works all things in all *persons*.

The word "varieties" occurs in each description. The Greek term can refer to either "distinctions" or "distributions." Relying on both senses of the term, we can say that the "varieties" of gifts are "distributed." As Paul presents his descriptions, he attaches one Person of the Godhead to each one. It is clear, however, that each description may be attributed to all three Persons. Any distinctions that exist are primarily rhetorical.

First, in verse 4, Paul says, "There are varieties of gifts (*charismatōn*), but the same Spirit." Here, the distributor of the gifts is the Holy Spirit. The term *charismatōn* stresses the grace ("charis") of God. The gifts of the Spirit are distributed to us, not because of our worthiness, but because of God's love for us and the people to whom we minister by means of these gifts.

Second, in verse 5, Paul says, "There are varieties of ministries (*diakoniōn*), and the same Lord." Here, Paul uses the Greek word *diakoniōn* to describe the gifts. The word is correctly translated "ministries." Here, Jesus as Lord is the distributor of the gifts. Jesus is the Lord of the ministries and the ministers. Furthermore, He ministers and serves through us.

Third, in verse 6, Paul says, "There are varieties of effects (*energēmatōn*), but the same God who works (*energōn*) all things in all persons." The Greek word *energōn* can mean "operate," "perform," or "energize." We take our English word "energy" from the Greek word. God the Father energizes us through His bestowal of the gifts upon us. Because of His energizing, we are effective in our work. In verse 11, Paul says that the Spirit "works (*energei*) all these things, distributing to each one individually just as He wills."

Paul identifies the source of the gifts in two other verses (1 Cor. 12:7, 28). With another expression, he again attributes the gifts to the Spirit. He writes, "To each one is given the manifestation (*phanerōsis*) of the Spirit" (v. 7). Although "manifestation of the Spirit" can mean "that which manifests the Spirit" or "the manifestation which the Spirit produces," the context (vv. 3, 4, 8, 9, 11) favors the latter. The Spirit distributes spiritual gifts to us. These gifts are the manifestations inspired by the Spirit. In verse 28, Paul states that God "has appointed" the gifts in the church.

3. *Natural or Supernatural.* The gifts of the Spirit vary somewhat in whether they are natural or supernatural. For example, the gift of "helps" is listed (1 Cor. 12:28) right in the same list with miracles, gifts of healings, and various types of tongues. It is easy for us to think of "helps' as largely a manifestation of natural abilities. We must keep in mind that even natural abilities are gifts from God (James 1:17). Moreover, it sometimes takes a lot of God's grace to keep on helping when others do not. So God enhances our natural talent with His grace. On the other hand, other gifts seem purely supernatural, such as miracles and gifts of healings.

4. *Overlapping gifts.* We should not attempt to define each gift too precisely and narrowly. The gifts of the Spirit overlap in function. For example, the word of knowledge, the word of wisdom, prophecy, and revelation are all interrelated. Each term has its own emphasis, but each of them deals with communicating truth under the inspiration of the Spirit. As another example, the gift of helps can encompass many gifts. All of the gifts are for the benefit and "help" of the body of Christ.

5. *Body of Christ.* Spiritual gifts and the body of Christ are closely related subjects. The body of Christ is mentioned several times in connection with spiritual gifts (Rom. 12:4–5; 1 Cor. 12:4–7, 27; Eph. 4:4–6). Spiritual gifts are bestowed within the body; that is, they are given to members of the body. Moreover, the gifts are given "for the common good" (1 Cor. 12:7). Through the gifts, we are enabled to enlarge, care for, and edify the body of Christ.

The gifts are very different and, even within the church, they are exercised in different settings. For example, the gift of administration is exercised in the daily ongoing work of the church. The gift of prophecy is expressed in the worship service itself. The gift of "helps" can be anywhere: in the worship service, out on the parking lot, in the foyer, during hospital visitation, and anywhere else at any time.

The Church Service

Should the gifts of the Spirit be exercised in the church worship service? When this question is asked, it often seems that the gifts in mind are the vocal gifts such as speaking in tongues, interpretation of tongues, word of knowledge, word of wisdom, and prophecy. The issue may be whether or not newcomers will consider the operation of the gifts very strange and will be put off. The answer to this has to do with the vision of the pastor and congregation as to the type of church they want to be. However, even when expression of these gifts is desired, there are questions of order and procedure.

As background for an answer to our question, consider the example of a church service that Paul gives us. In 1 Corinthians 14:26–33, Paul deals with edifying participation in the corporate worship of the church. Here, he describes how the worship service should flow. He tells what a service characterized by participation would look like.

> [26]What is the outcome then, brethren? When you assemble, each one has a psalm, has a teaching, has a revelation, has a tongue, has an interpretation. Let all things be done for edification. [27]If anyone speaks in a tongue, it should be by two or at the most three, and each in turn, and one must interpret; [28]but if there is no interpreter, he must keep silent in the church; and let him speak to himself and to God. [29]Let two or three prophets speak, and let the others pass judgment. [30]But if a revelation is made to another who is seated, the first one must keep silent. [31]For you can all prophesy one by one, so that all may learn and all may be exhorted; [32]and the spirits of prophets are subject to prophets; [33]for God is not a God of confusion but of peace, as in all the churches of the saints.

It seems obvious that the early church service was highly participatory. No doubt this was why Paul cautioned the church about the amount and order of participation. If there were no participation, there would be no need for guidance. The assembled believers did not come expecting to just sit quietly and observe what was going on. Each one had a participatory role.

1. *Preparation.* When people came to the worship service in the early church, they came with their hearts prepared to participate. Some came (v. 26) with content, such as a psalm, a teaching, or a revelation prepared. This may have been true of tongues and interpretation as well. However, much of the content (v. 30) was inspired, no doubt, during the service. Even though their participation was spontaneous, their hearts were prepared for the participation.

Some aspects of this particular pattern may not fit every circumstance. For example, it is not possible in a very large group that each one will come with a psalm or teaching. The service would be unending. So, this pattern seems to fit a group that is relatively small. However, when managed properly, there can be participation in a large audience as well. The validity of preparing for this interpretation permits an orderly approach to the exercise of the gifts. Although the manner in which gifts are expressed may vary, it is important that the Spirit move mightily among us.

2. *Tongues and Interpretation.* In verses 27–28, Paul gives several guidelines regarding tongues and interpretation. One view of these verses is that there should not be more than two or three utterances in tongues before an interpretation. Another view is that there should not be more than two or three utterances in tongues in any given service. Each of these utterances should be followed, in turn, by an interpretation. The clause "when you assemble" suggests than in any given service, the tongues and interpretation should be limited to two or three. Therefore, the second approach above seems to be better. The main point, however, is that there should be balanced participation. There were other gifts to express besides tongues and interpretation.

In verse 28, it is assumed that someone other than the speaker in tongues will interpret. Apparently, the speaker in tongues, and perhaps the entire congregation, was to know whether or not an interpreter was present. The speaker in tongues could pray (v. 13), alternatively, that he might interpret. If he, or someone else, were not prepared to interpret, he was to keep silent and speak to himself and to God. This speaking might be in the form of thinking within himself, but the prayer might be quietly vocalized as well.

3. *Prophecy.* In verses 29–32, the apostle gives guidelines for prophecy as well. Many believe that only two or three prophets should speak in any given service. This view allows for the passing of judgment to be prophecy-by-prophecy or after two or three prophetic words. No doubt, some judged silently even while the prophet was speaking. Another view is that only two or three should speak before others pass judgment. Several points attract our attention.

First, the "others" are to pass judgment. This could mean that only those who have the prophetic gift should judge, but we note that "all" can potentially prophesy. Moreover, in verse 24, all are involved in judging the unbeliever. To pass judgment means to "weigh carefully" the content of the prophecies given.

Second, while a prophet is speaking, a "revelation" may come to another person. Although prophecy is a broader term than revelation, many prophecies are based on revelation. Here, Paul exhorts the first prophet to make way for the one who has just received a revelation. Those who prophesy must recognize the gifts of others.

Third, with regard to verse 32, one view is that each prophet must be subject to other prophets. A second view is that each prophet is in control of his own spirit. Another view is that "spirits of the prophets" refers to "the prophetic Spirit." In this case, the prophetic Spirit would speak through the spirit of the prophet. Given Paul's emphasis on the inspiration of the Spirit, this view is best.

Conclusion

As believers in Christ, we have the privilege of a very close relationship with the Triune God. God dwells in us, and we dwell in Him. The Spirit of God exalts Christ and applies His redemptive work to us. He helps us grow and develop the fruit of the Spirit so that we are like Christ in our attitudes and relationships with others. In addition, the Spirit gives us gifts that enable us to minister out of love in an effective manner to the body of Christ. Let us manifest both the gifts and the fruit of the Spirit.

CHAPTER TEN

TAKING "NOT YET" SERIOUSLY

Whether or not Christians need to develop in their spiritual lives is not in debate. All believers recognize that they have more to learn, more to experience, and more to overcome. We have not yet arrived!

The apostle Paul recognized that there were spiritual things he had not already obtained. He did not think that he had already laid hold of or seized them. As a result, he was determined to press on in his relationship with God. His attitude is appropriate for all believers. Paul states a general principle about our relationship with God in Philippians 3:12–14.

> [12]Not that I have already obtained it or have already become perfect, but I press on so that I may lay hold of that for which also I was laid hold of by Christ Jesus. [13]Brethren, I do not regard myself as having laid hold of it yet; but one thing I do: forgetting what lies behind and reaching forward to what lies ahead, [14]I press on toward the goal for the prize of the upward call of God in Christ Jesus.

Obviously this general principle applies to all aspects of our spiritual growth, including our relationship with the Holy Spirit. It is through the Spirit that we are developed in the image of Christ and reach full stature.

When we come to Christ, we are given the position of sons of God, and the Spirit does His initial work. Thereafter, we begin to experience all that we have as sons. We can never say that we have fully arrived. Rather, we always continue to grow and to experience more of the presence and power of God. The Holy Spirit continues His relationship with us and works within and through us. As maturing believers, we must take "not yet" seriously!

Becoming What We Are

The apostle Paul writes this declaration to the Corinthians: "And such were some of you, but you were washed, but you were sanctified, but you were justified in the name of the Lord Jesus Christ, and in the Spirit of our God" (1 Cor. 6:11). Although all of these actions point to our position in Christ, we must apply all of these actions to our lives. We must become what we are.

1. *Sets of Terms.* Our life in Christ begins when we believe in Him, and it is fully developed over time. Scholars describe this truth with several sets of terms. Underlying all of these sets of terms is the premise that we are becoming what we already are.

- God establishes our *position* as sons, and then we *experience* all that it means to be a son. When we believe in Christ, we become sons of God. Because we are sons, God sends the Spirit into our hearts to give us assurance of our standing (Gal. 4:6).
- God accepts us in an *objective* sense, and then we have *subjective* experience. What God has objectively done for believers, they subjectively experience now and will have fuller experience in the future. Although believers have already benefited both objectively and subjectively by the saving activity of God, they will more fully experience the power of the age to come at the second coming of Christ.
- We are *potentially* what we can become, and we *actually* become that in our experience over time. When believers come to Christ, they are potentially all that they can ever become. We see this, for example, with regard to positional and experiential sanctification. We progressively realize our positional sanctification.
- Some expositors speak about the *indicative* and the *imperative* moods. The indicative mood refers to what already exists in our spiritual lives, while the imperative mood calls us to what we must still appropriate. For example, we have been baptized in water (Rom. 6:3–4), but we must walk in newness of life.
- We *already* have our spiritual inheritance, but we have *not yet* appropriated it all. Usually the term "already" is applied to the great historical work of Christ in redemption. The "not yet" part of the expression applies to what is still to be accomplished. All aspects of our salvation are included.

In my view, we can apply this expression to our subjective experience as well. As believers, we have subjectively experienced much, but there is always more. Thus, we can refer to the work that the Spirit has "already" done in us, but yet believe He will do more.

2. *Three Tenses*. With this as a background, the central principle of Paul's thought emerges. This central principle is that salvation is in three tenses—past, present, and future. When individuals believe in Christ, they are already saved; but they are still being saved, and their ultimate salvation is yet future. They must become what they already are in Christ. What God has objectively done, they must experience subjectively. Moreover, they must realize the unrealized power of the age to come in their lives. Although greater realization is possible now, the full realization of their salvation is yet future.

3. *Vocabulary*. Much biblical interpretation is based on "either-or" thinking about definitions of words. Each writer takes one side or the other. Some of the terms, it is held, are descriptive of the initial reception of the Spirit, while others relate to subsequent experiences. However, given Paul's comprehensive mind and his "already–not yet" mode of thought, we can often include both aspects at the same time. Some of what he says presupposes a complete experience in all dimensions.

Paul's vocabulary concerning our life in the Spirit is full and varied. When we come to faith in Christ, the promise of the Spirit begins to be realized. We continue to receive the supply of the Spirit throughout our lives. We will realize the presence and work of the Spirit fully in the future. We do not need to define terms narrowly, such as being "anointed." These terms have a full background of usage and can apply to us in a variety of ways. Our attention should focus on having a current and living relationship with the Holy Spirit. His presence and work will greatly enhance our lives.

Ministers

The grand design of God is to develop a body of believers which is "conformed to the image of His Son, that he might be the firstborn among many brethren" (Rom 8:29). To accomplish this purpose, God uses all things and makes all things work together. Nevertheless, it is primarily though human instruments endued with His power that He has chosen to work. Thus, people who minister have a vital part in guiding the saints to maturity in Christ. They are partners with God, albeit junior partners, in achieving His goal.

1. *Workers Together.* The church is blessed with ministers called of God to teach, strengthen, and comfort the saints. As ministers, we work with God to lead men to Christ and to help them grow in His likeness. The mutual efforts of God and man extend to all phases of this task, including bringing children up in the nurture and admonition of the Lord, and leading older people to keep growing. We are workers together with God to accomplish the goal of presenting every man complete in Christ (Col. 1:28–29). As Paul says:

> [28]We proclaim Him, admonishing every man and teaching every man with all wisdom, so that we may present every man complete in Christ. [29]For this purpose also I labor, striving according to His power, which mightily works within me.

In working with God to bring the body of Christ to maturity, we strive to help everyone we can. We must remember, however, that we are striving with the energy which God supplies to us. His energy will be sufficient for the task.

2. *Training Workers.* Also, teachers can train the saints so that they in turn can minister to others and bring them to spiritual maturity. Such training consists of perfecting the trainees spiritually and equipping them for their ministries. This is why God gave His ministers to the church. They lead us on to higher heights. Paul (Eph. 4:11–13) wrote:

> [11]And He gave some *as* apostles, and some *as* prophets, and some *as* evangelists, and some *as* pastors and teachers, [12]for the equipping of the saints for the work of service, to the building up of the body of Christ; [13]until we all attain to the unity of the faith, and of the knowledge of the Son of God, to a mature man, to the measure of the stature which belongs to the fullness of Christ.

A key phrase in this passage is "for the equipping of the saints for the work of service." This phrase focuses on the task of training the saints so that they can do the work of the ministry. They are the ones who, along with us, will help build up the body of Christ. We cannot do the task alone, but we must be able to train an army of workers to do the job.

3. *Holy Spirit*. The Holy Spirit empowers us in all aspects of our ministry. In 1 Thessalonians 1:5, Paul says, "For our gospel did not come to you in word only, but also in power and in the Holy Spirit and with full conviction." As teachers and trainers, we rely fully on the Holy Spirit. Also, as we labor, we can model Spirit-inspired ministry to others who will follow us.

Models of Spiritual Development

Three models of spiritual development can be derived from the Scriptures. First is the encounter model. We develop in our spiritual lives by encounters, or crisis experiences, in the Spirit. Second, another model has to do with spiritual growth. The growth model emphasizes continuous experience. We keep on growing as we relate to the Spirit. Third, the inclusive model stresses that we relate to the Spirit through both crisis experiences and ongoing growth. All of these models are important for our spiritual development.

1. *Encounter Model*. We develop in our spiritual lives by encounters, or crisis experiences, in the Spirit. On the Day of Pentecost (Acts 2:4), the disciples had a crisis experience of the Spirit. It was an observable experience that they could know they had. This was true at Caesarea (Acts 10:44–46) and Ephesus (Acts 19:1–6) as well. The special benefit in these cases was empowerment for witness and service.

When Paul was in Ephesus, he asked the disciples an experiential question (Acts 19:2): "He said to them, 'Did you receive the Holy Spirit when you believed?' And they said to him, 'No, we have not even heard whether there is a Holy Spirit.'" Upon hearing their answer, Paul baptized them in water. When Paul laid his hands on them, the Holy Spirit came upon them, and they spoke in tongues and prophesied. Many scholars try to deemphasize this experience. Some say the story is redacted by Luke, and that it is not Pauline. Taken at face value, this story simply describes Paul in action.

2. *Growth Model*. The growth model emphasizes continuous experience. We keep on growing as we relate to the Spirit. The apostle Paul says: "But we all, with unveiled face, beholding as in a

mirror the glory of the Lord, are being transformed into the same image from glory to glory, just as from the Lord, the Spirit" (2 Cor. 3:18). The ongoing spiritual development of the saints is essential.

In Romans 12:2, the apostle Paul says, "And do not be conformed to this world, but be transformed by the renewing of your mind, so that you may prove what the will of God is, that which is good and acceptable and perfect." As we live for the Lord, He transforms us in every aspect of our lives.

3. *Inclusive Model.* The inclusive model stresses that we relate to the Spirit through both crisis experiences and ongoing growth. In other words, we cannot rely on one model without the other. For some people, the encounter model is the one that counts most; for others, the growth model is paramount, if not the exclusive model that matters. The Bible includes both in the inclusive model.

A crisis experience alone is not sufficient in the development of spiritual life. We must continue to grow. However, some people ask this question: Can a believer arrive at the same place spiritually through the growth model without a crisis experience as he does through both crisis and growth? In other words, does a crisis experience have unique value not obtainable through growth? As I see it, the crisis experience has value in itself. This value varies somewhat for each individual. Most people, though, testify to the great sense of empowerment that is gained through a crisis experience.

Aspects of Growth

The baptism in the Spirit as an event is important; but it is essential, also, that believers experience the Spirit in His various ongoing dimensions. All of the dimensions of the Spirit in the Bible are important. Believers develop in their experience through all the above models of spiritual life. Now let us consider many of the aspects of growth that we can experience.

1. *John's Writings.* John emphasized the abiding presence of the Spirit in the life of the believer, eternal life by the quickening of the Spirit, the Spirit of Truth, the role of the Spirit in maturity and ministry, and the Spirit who speaks. When we review the writings of John, several areas of spiritual growth and development stand out.

First, God has offered us abundant life through Christ. That abundant life touches us in every aspect of our living. Jesus said, "The thief comes only to steal and kill and destroy; I came that they may have life, and have *it* abundantly" (John 10:10). It is supremely important to experience spiritual life in abundant measure. As we live for Christ, we can continue to deepen our experience and to know Christ better. At the same time, believers often are greatly blessed in material things. As Jesus said, "But seek first His kingdom and His righteousness; and all these things shall be added unto you" (Matt. 6:33).

Second, we should grow in our knowledge and understanding of truth. Jesus declared, "And you shall know the truth, and the truth shall make you free" (John 8:32). The Spirit will guide us into all truth, so we should be candidates for growth. Jesus said, "But when He, the Spirit of truth, comes, He will guide you into all the truth; for He will not speak on His own initiative, but whatever He hears, He will speak; and He will disclose to you what is to come" (John 16:13). We must keep on learning things to come. Moreover, we can grow in our ability to worship Jesus in Spirit and truth. Jesus said, "God is spirit, and those who worship Him must worship in spirit and truth" (John 4:24).

Third, we continue to grow in our relationship with Christ. Jesus proclaimed, "My sheep hear My voice, and I know them, and they follow Me" (John 10:27). We can be so close to Jesus that it is easy to hear His voice. Jesus dwells in us (John 17:23). John writes, "His anointing teaches you about all things" (1 John 2:27). The Spirit teaches us, and we grow in knowledge.

Fourth, we must witness boldly. During the evening of resurrection day, Jesus breathed on the disciples and bestowed the Spirit. Then, He made a highly significant comment about their witness: "If you forgive the sins of any, *their sins* have been forgiven them; if you retain the *sins* of any, they have been retained" (John 20:23). The disciples did not have an independent power to forgive and retain sins. They did so by proclaiming the Gospel. When people accepted the Gospel, God would forgive them; and when they rejected the Gospel, God would retain their sins. They would not be forgiven. Given our responsibility to proclaim the Gospel, we must constantly grow in our witness.

2. *Luke's Writings*. In chapter 6, I presented an overview of the dimensions of the Spirit described in Luke's writings. When the body of Christ is empowered, one can expect that it will have a sense of mission, that it will be guided by the Spirit, that the Spirit will reveal Himself in special ways, that there will be dreams and visions, that there will be miracles, and that there will be joy over the progress of the kingdom of God.

First, when Philip preached the "good news about the kingdom of God and the name of Jesus Christ" (Acts 8:12), many of the Samaritans believed. Then they were baptized in water. The news was reported to the church in Jerusalem, and Peter and John were sent to Samaria to help the disciples take a forward step. Luke tells us the reason why they were sent. He declares, "For He [the Holy Spirit] had not yet fallen upon any of them; they had simply been baptized in the name of the Lord Jesus" (Acts 8:16). Peter and John helped the disciples know the importance of a crisis experience of the presence of the Spirit. When they laid hands on the believers and prayed, the Spirit came upon the disciples in an observable way.

Even after the Spirit comes upon us in a dramatic way, we must be open to repeated and continuous experience in the Spirit. We must continue to take the phrase "not yet" seriously. We can always enrich our relationship with the Holy Spirit. He is present with us, yet He can be more powerfully present. So we must always be open to a stronger connection.

Second, all individual believers should be empowered to witness. All should be filled with the Spirit. There is considerable variety, though, with regard to how the Spirit works through each individual life. Not all have dreams and visions. Not all have revelations. Not all do mighty and miraculous deeds. Much like the variety there is in the distribution of the gifts of the Spirit (1 Cor. 12:4–11), there is variety in the realization of the Lucan dimensions of the Spirit. However, all believers should seek to be used mightily by God as He wills.

Third, a very dominant emphasis in Luke, both before and after Pentecost, is on the guidance by the Holy Spirit. Sometimes that guidance included a revelation from the Spirit about relevant circumstances. Today, witnesses are to be guided and led by the Spirit. May believers today always be sensitive to His leadership!

One, the Spirit guided the early church with regard to decisions affecting spiritual life. The apostles, elders, and the whole church sent a letter from the Jerusalem Council to the church in Antioch, declaring, "For it seemed good to the Holy Spirit and to us to lay upon you no greater burden than these essentials" (Acts 15:28). Luke does not tell how the Spirit made His wisdom known to the church, but He did so. Led by the Spirit, the church had made the decision that circumcision would not be required. It was important to the church that they were led by the Spirit.

Two, Luke describes the role of the Holy Spirit in selecting and appointing leaders. In Acts 13:2, he says, "While they [the prophets and teachers] were ministering to the Lord and fasting, the Holy Spirit said, 'Set apart for Me Barnabas and Saul for the work to which I have called them.'" Because the Holy Spirit had called Barnabas and Saul, the prophets and teachers were to set them apart. Luke does not state exactly how the Holy Spirit spoke, and one can only surmise that He spoke to the prophets who were with Barnabas and Saul. It may be that He spoke through one of them with a prophetic word.

During his farewell speech at Ephesus, Paul tells the elders that the Holy Spirit "has made you overseers" (Acts 20:28). Whatever human process was involved in their rising to leadership, the real appointment was made by the Spirit. They were chosen to shepherd the church of God. The Spirit obviously led in the selection of the overseers.

Three, when Philip was on the road from Jerusalem to Gaza (Acts 8:26), he encountered the chariot of the Ethiopian eunuch. Luke says, "Then the Spirit said to Philip, 'Go up and join this chariot'" (8:29). A conversation between Philip and the eunuch ensued, resulting in the Ethiopian being baptized. Now Luke says, "When they came up out of the water, the Spirit of the Lord snatched Philip away; and the eunuch no longer saw him, but went on his way rejoicing" (8:39). The "snatching away" was a very unusual occurrence.

Three verses have to do with how the Spirit led Peter with regard to his ministry to the Gentiles at Caesarea. In his vision concerning eating animals (Acts 10:9–16), a voice told Peter, "What God has cleansed, no longer consider unholy" (v. 15). Then, "While Peter was reflecting on the vision, the Spirit said to him, 'Behold, three men are looking for you. But arise, go downstairs, and accompany them without misgivings; for I have sent them Myself'" (Acts 10:19–20). Then, in Acts 11:12, when Peter was telling the story, he repeated what the Spirit said, stating, "The Spirit told me to go with them without misgivings."

The apostle Paul and his companions were also led of the Spirit. In Acts 13:4, Luke says, "So being sent out by the Holy Spirit, they went down to Seleucia and from there they sailed to Cyprus." Concerning another time, he writes, "They passed through the Phrygian and Galatian region, having been forbidden by the Holy Spirit to speak the word in Asia; and after they came to Mysia, they were trying to go into Bithynia, and the Spirit of Jesus did not permit them" (Acts 16:6–7). Thus, the Spirit not only guides people to certain places, but He also prevents them from going to some places.

3. *Paul's Writings.* Paul's presentation of the Spirit is very comprehensive. In chapter three, I discussed the works of the Spirit in salvation, including regeneration, justification, adoption, and sanctification. Each of these works has its ongoing realization. In addition, Paul focuses on such ongoing dimensions as the fruit of the Spirit and gifts of the Spirit.

First, the apostle Paul applies this principle to adoption. In Romans 8:15, Paul says that we "have received a spirit of adoption as sons by which we cry out, 'Abba! Father!'" Then, in Romans 8:23, Paul declares that "we ourselves, having the first fruits of the Spirit, even we ourselves groan within ourselves, waiting eagerly for our adoption as sons, the redemption of our body." Although it is primarily the Father who adopts, the term "Spirit of adoption" indicates that the Spirit has a role in adoption. The works of the Spirit continue throughout the believer's life.

Second, the phrase "first fruits of the Spirit" can be interpreted to refer to the Holy Spirit as we know Him now. The rest of the fruit will be the Spirit as we will know Him in the future. Or, the first fruits could be the initial work of the Spirit, and the rest of the fruit could be the future works of the Spirit. Even if this view be true, it just means that Paul does not distinguish sharply between the Spirit and His works. The Spirit in the life of the believer is present in His works. Because "first fruits" is a harvest term, it is best to assume the rest of the harvest will be of the same kind. For this reason, I favor the first view above. However, the future harvest of the Spirit includes His works on behalf of believers.

Third, one must be spiritually renewed. Throughout the Christian walk, the believer is renewed in all aspects of salvation. Concerning renewal, Paul said to the Romans, "And do not be conformed to this world, but be transformed by the renewing of your mind, that you may prove what the will of God is, that which is good and acceptable and perfect" (12:2). Spiritual renewal is experienced in many different ways: with wonderful event-type experiences, growing almost imperceptibly, or by living in a state of renewal.

Fourth, the same principle applies to the fruit of the Spirit. While writing to the Galatians, Paul listed these fruit of the Spirit: "But the fruit of the Spirit is love, joy, peace, patience, kindness, goodness, faithfulness, gentleness, self-control" (5:22–23). Then, he said, "If we live by the Spirit, let us also walk by the Spirit" (5:26). The Spirit not only gives new life; He also helps manifest the fruit of the Spirit in the believer's walk.

The fruit of the Spirit are essential to healthy Christian living. Take, for example, the fruit of love. One reason love is so important is that it is a characteristic that will distinguish believers as Christians. In John 13:35, Jesus says, "By this all men will know that you are My disciples, if you have love for one another." One's love is not always constant. As human individuals, it varies in intensity. The believer must pray always that the Spirit keeps love alive in his or her heart.

Fifth, with regard to the gifts of the Spirit, Paul said, "But earnestly desire the greater gifts. And I show you a still more excellent way" (1 Cor. 12:31). Believers are exhorted to desire the greater gifts, but they must desire the gifts for the right reason. The more excellent way is to exercise the gifts through love for the benefit of the body of Christ. Believers must not be passive about this. If they truly love others, they will desire to be used of God in every possible way to meet needs.

Conclusion

As believers in Christ, we are on a wonderful spiritual journey. The journey began when we accepted Christ through faith. It has continued ever since. When we abide in Christ, all of the experiences of life contribute to our development. Even times of adversity have their positive impact in the long run. Then, there are many moments of open and positive blessing that give us great spiritual enjoyment.

Our lives are devoted not only to reaching "full stature" but also to reaching, teaching, and training others. They, in turn, will grow in the image of Christ and help to training a growing body of believers who will be engaged in the work of the kingdom of God. Our relationship with the Holy Spirit is an essential part of making our spiritual journey the very best that it can be. We are becoming what we are.

SCRIPTURE INDEX

GREEK TERMS TRANSLITERATED

The transliteration of each Greek term is listed first below. If that term is not the lexical form, that form is given in parentheses before the page numbers where the terms appear in the text. The terms are alphabetized according to the English transliteration, not according to the order found in the Greek alphabet.

agesthe (agō), 108

anabainō, 6

apostellō, 6, 42, 52

baptisei (baptizō) , 5

baptizō, 52

baptizōn (baptizō), 5

bebaiōn (bebaioō), 61

charin (charis), 112

charismata (charisma), 111, 112

charismatōn (charisma), 112, 113

chriō, 52

chrisas (chriō), 49

chrisma, 52

diakoniōn (diakonia), 113

didōmi, 52

didonta (didōmi), 44

didōsin (didōmi), 43

domata (doma), 111, 112

echei (echō), 29, 41, 60

echō, 52

eis 30, 95

ekcheō, 52

elabete (lambanō), 46

elegxei (elegchō, elenchō), 19

elegchetai (elegchō, elenchō), 17

en, 4, 5, 30, 95

energēmatōn (energēma), 113

energōn (energeō), 113

enoikeō, 52

enoikountos (enoikeō), 60

eperchomai, 52

epichorēgias (epichorēgeō), 61

epichorēgōn (epichorēgeō), 45, 60

epipiptō, 52

eplērounto (plēroō), 47

epotisthemen (potizō), 30

erchomai, 52

estai (eimi), 4

exapesteilen (exapostellō), 43

exapostellō, 52

helkusēi (helkuō),14

helkusō (helkuō), 14

hoti , 19, 20, 22

hupsoō, 8

hupsōtheis (hupsoō), 8

katoikeō, 52

lambanō, 52

labōn (lambanō), 8

meizona (megas), 112

COMPREHENSIVE BIBLIOGRAPHY
ON THE HOLY SPIRIT

Allen, Roland. 1962. *The Ministry of the Spirit*. Grand Rapids: Wm. B. Eerdmans.

Anderson, Robert Mapes. 1979. *Vision of the Disinherited*. Oxford: Oxford University Press.

Archer, Gleason L., Jr. 1974. *A Survey of Old Testament Introduction*. Chicago: Moody Press.

Arndt, William F., F. Wilbur Gingrich, Frederick W. Danker, and Walter Bauer. 1979. *A Greek–English Lexicon of the New Testament and Other Early Christian Literature*. Chicago: University of Chicago Press.

Arrington, French L. 1988. *The Acts of the Apostles*. Peabody, MA: Hendrickson Publishers.

Arthur, William. 1919. *The Tongue of Fire*. Nashville: Publishing House of the M. E. Church.

Baker, D. L. 1976. *Two Testaments, One Bible*. Leicester: Inter–Varsity Press.

Baker, John. 1967. *Baptized in One Spirit*. Plainfield: Logos Books.

Barclay, William. 1956. *The Gospel of John, Volume 1*. Philadelphia: The Westminster Press.

Barnes, Albert. 1983. *Barnes's Notes*. Grand Rapids: Baker Book House.

Barrett, C. K. 1966. *The Holy Spirit and the Gospel Tradition*. London: SPCK.

—————. 1971a. *A Commentary on the Epistle to the Romans*. London: Adam and Charles Black.

—————. 1971b. *A Commentary on the First Epistle to the Corinthians*. 2. ed. London: Adam and Charles Black.

—————. 1973. *A Commentary on the Second Epistle to the Corinthians*. 2. ed. London: Adam and Charles Black.

—————. 1978. *The Gospel According to St. John*. Philadelphia: The Westminster Press.

Beare, Francis W. 1953. *The Epistle to the Ephesians. The Interpreter's Bible, Vol. IX*. New York: Abingdon Press.

Beasley–Murray, G. R. n.d. *II Corinthians. The Broadman Bible Commentary, Vol. 11. 2 Corinthians–Philemon*. Ed. Clifton J. Allen. Nashville: Broadman Press.

—————. 1962. *Baptism in the New Testament*. Grand Rapids: Wm. B. Eerdmans.

—————. 1986. *Jesus and the Kingdom of God*. Grand Rapids: Wm. B. Eerdmans.

Bennett, Dennis J. 1970. *Nine O'Clock in the Morning*. Plainfield: Logos International.

Bennett, Dennis, and Rita Bennett. 1971. *The Holy Spirit and You*. Plainfield: Logos International.

Berding, Kenneth. 2006. *What Are Spiritual Gifts?* Grand Rapids: Kregel Publications.

Berkhof, Hendrikus. 1964. *The Doctrine of the Holy Spirit*. Atlanta: John Knox Press.

Bickersteth, Edward Henry. 1959. *The Holy Spirit*. Grand Rapids: Kregel Publications.

Biederwolf, William Edward. 1964. *The Millennium Bible*. Grand Rapids: Baker Book House.

—————. 1974. *A Help to the Study of the Holy Spirit*. Grand Rapids: Baker Book House.

Blaising, Craig A., and Darrell L. Bock. 1992. *Dispensationalism, Israel and the Church*. Ed. Darrell L. Grand Rapids: Zondervan.

—————. 1993. *Progressive Dispensationalism*. Wheaton: Victor Books.

Boer, Harry R. 1961. *Pentecost and Missions*. Grand Rapids: Wm. B. Eerdmans.

Boyd, Frank M. 1951. *Book of the Prophet Ezekiel*. Springfield, MO: Gospel Publishing House.

—————. 1970. *The Spirit Works Today*. Springfield, MO: Gospel Publishing House.

Brandt, R. L. 1981. *Charismatics: Are We Missing Something?* Plainfield: Logos International.

Brown, Ramond E. 1966. *The Gospel According to John*. 2 vols. *Anchor Bible 29, 29A*. Garden City: New York: Doubleday.

Bruce, F. F. 1963. *The Epistle of Paul to the Romans*. Grand Rapids: Wm. B. Eerdmans.

—————. 1975. *The Book of Acts*. Grand Rapids: Wm. B. Eerdmans.

—————. 1984. *The Epistles to the Colossians, to Philemon, and to the Ephesians*. Grand Rapids: Wm. B. Eerdmans.

Brumback, Carl. 1947. *"What Meaneth This?"* Springfield, MO: Gospel Publishing House.

Bruner, Frederick Dale. 1970. *A Theology of the Holy Spirit.* Grand Rapids: Wm. B. Eerdmans.

Bullock, C. Hassell. 1986. *An Introduction to the Old Testament Prophetic Books.* Chicago: Moody Press.

Bultmann, Rudolf. 1952. *Theology of the New Testament.* 2 Vols. London: SCM Press Ltd.

Burdick, Donald W. 1969. *Tongues: To Speak or Not To Speak.* Chicago: Moody Press.

Burge, Gary M. 1987. *The Anointed Community: The Holy Spirit in the Johannine Tradition.* Grand Rapids: Wm. B. Eerdmans.

—————. 1996. *The Letters of John: The NIV Application Commentary.* Grand Rapids: Zondervan.

Burgess, Stanley M. 1984. *The Spirit and the Church: Antiquity.* Peabody, MA: Hendrickson Publishers.

Burton, Ernest DeWitt. 1976. *Syntax of the Moods and Tenses in New Testament Greek.* Grand Rapids: Kregel Publications.

Calvin, John. 1960. *Calvin's Commentaries. The First Epistle of Paul the Apostle to the Corinthians.* Trans. John W. Fraser. Grand Rapids: Wm. B. Eerdmans.

Cantelon, Willard. 1951. *The Baptism in the Holy Spirit.* Springfield, MO: Gospel Publishing House.

Carson, D. A. 1984. *Exegetical Fallacies.* Grand Rapids: Baker Book House.

Carter, Charles W. 1974. *The Person and Ministry of the Holy Spirit.* Grand Rapids: Baker Book House.

Carter, Howard. 1976. *Questions and Answers on Spiritual Gifts.* Tulsa: Harrison House.

Chafer, Lewis Sperry. 1948. *Systematic Theology.* Vol. VI. Dallas: Dallas Seminary Press.

Chapman, Colin. 1989. *Whose Promised Land?* Oxford: Lion Publishing.

—————. 1992. *Whose Promised Land?* Oxford: Lion Publishing.

Chase, Alston Hurd, and Henry Phillips. 1949. *A New Introduction to Greek.* Cambridge: Harvard University Press.

Christenson, Larry. 1963. *The Gift of Tongues.* Minneapolis: Bethany Fellowship.

—————. 1972. *A Message to the Charismatic Movement.* Minneapolis: Bethany Fellowship.

—————. 1968. *Speaking in Tongues.* Minneapolis: Bethany Fellowship.

Clarke, Adam. n.d. *The Old Testament, Vol. I.—Genesis to Deuteronomy*. New York: Abingdon–Cokesbury Press.

————. n.d. *The New Testament, Vol. I.—Matthew to the Acts*. New York: Abingdon–Cokesbury Press.

————. n.d. *The New Testament, Vol. II.—Romans to the Revelation*. New York: Abingdon–Cokesbury Press.

Cockburn, Ian. 1971. *Baptism in the Holy Spirit*. Plainfield: Logos International.

Cole, R. Alan. 1965. *The Epistle of Paul to the Galatians*. Grand Rapids: Wm. B. Eerdmans.

Collins, Michael. 1974. *Baptisms*. Midland Road: Students Pentecostal Fellowship.

Conn, Charles W. 1956. *Pillars of Pentecost*. Cleveland: The Pathway Press.

Conzelmann, Hans. 1957. *The Theology of St Luke*. London: SCM Press.

Criswell, W. A. 1966. *The Holy Spirit in Today's World*. Grand Rapids: Zondervan.

Crockett, William V., and James G. Sigountos, eds. 1991. *Through No Fault of Their Own*. Grand Rapids: Baker Book House.

Cullman, Oscar. 1950. *Baptism in the New Testament*. Philadelphia: The Westminster Press.

Cumming, James Elder. 1965. *Through the Eternal Spirit*. Minneapolis: Bethany Fellowship.

Cummings, Robert. 1948. *"Unto You Is the Promise."* Springfield, MO: Gospel Publishing House.

Dale, James W. 1867. *Classic Baptism*. Philadelphia: Sherman and Co..

Davidson, Leslie. 1971. *Pathway to Power*. Watchung: Charisma Books.

Deere, Jack. 1993. *Surprised by the Power of the Spirit*. Grand Rapids: Zondervan.

Dennis, J. A. n.d. *The Holy Spirit*. Austin: The Texas Herald.

Dumbrell, W. J. 1984. *Covenant and Creation*. Exeter: The Paternoster Press.

Dunn, James D. G. 1970. *Baptism in the Holy Spirit*. London: SCM Press Ltd.

————. 1975. *Jesus and the Spirit*. London: SCM Press Ltd.

Durasoff, Steve. 1972. *Bright Wind of the Holy Spirit: Pentecostalism Today*. Tulsa: RHEMA Bible Church.

Eichrodt, Walther. 1961. *Theology of the Old Testament, Volume 1*. Philadelphia: The Westminster Press.

————. 1967. *Theology of the Old Testament, Volume 2*. Philadelphia: The Westminster Press.

Erdman, Charles R. 1944. *The Gospel of John*. Philadelphia: The Westminster Press.

————. 1949. *The Gospel of Luke*. Philadelphia: The Westminster Press.

————. 1966. *The Epistles of Paul to the Thessalonians*. Philadelphia: The Westminster Press.

Erickson, Millard J. 1985. *Christian Theology*. Grand Rapids: Baker Book House.

Ervin, Howard M. 1968. *These Are Not Drunken as Ye Suppose*. Plainfield: Logos International.

————. 1971. *...And Forbid Not To Speak With Tongues*. Plainfield: Logos International.

————. 1972. *This Which Ye See And Hear*. Plainfield: Logos International, 1972.

————. 1984. *Conversion–Initiation and the Baptism in the Holy Spirit*. Peabody, MA: Hendrickson Publishers.

Evans, Tony. 1996. *The Promise*. Chicago: Moody Press.

Evans, W. I. 1954. *This River Must Flow*. Springfield, MO: Gospel Publishing House.

Ewert, David. 1983. *The Holy Spirit in the New Testament*. Scottdale: Herald Press.

Farrand, William. 1983. *Counselor, Teacher, and Guide: A Study on the Holy Spirit*. Brussels: International Correspondence Institute.

Fee, Gordon D. 1987. *The First Epistle to the Corinthians*. Grand Rapids: Wm. B. Eerdmans.

————. 1991. *Gospel and Spirit: Issues in New Testament Hermeneutics*. Peabody, MA: Hendrickson Publishers.

————. 1994. *God's Empowering Presence*. Peabody, MA: Hendrickson Publishers.

Fee, Gordon D., and Douglas Stuart. 1982. *How to Read the Bible for All Its Worth*. Grand Rapids: Academie Books.

Fernando, Ajith. 1998. *The NIV Application Commentary*. Grand Rapids: Zondervan.

Filson, Floyd V. 1953. *The Interpreter's Bible. The Second Epistle to the Corinthians*. New York: Abingdon Press.

Flattery, George M. 1968. *Teaching for Christian Maturity*. Springfield, MO: Gospel Publishing House.

Flynn, Leslie B. 1974. *19 Gifts of the Spirit.* Wheaton: Victor Books.

Foster, K. Neill. 1973. *A Revolution of Love.* Minneapolis: Bethany Fellowship.

Frost, Robert C. 1965. *Aglow with the Spirit.* Plainfield: Logos International.

————. 1971. *Overflowing Life.* Plainfield: Logos International.

————. 1973. *Set My Spirit Free.* Plainfield: Logos International.

Fung, Ronald Y. K. 1988. *The Epistle to the Galatians.* Grand Rapids: Wm. B. Eerdmans.

Gangel, Kenneth O. 1983. *Unwrap Your Spiritual Gifts.* Wheaton: Victor Books.

————. 1998. *Acts: Holman New Testament Commentary.* General Editor: Anders, Max. Nashville: Holman Reference.

Gee, Donald. 1949. *Concerning Spiritual Gifts.* Springfield, MO: Gospel Publishing House.

————. 1963. *Spiritual Gifts in the Work of the Ministry Today.* Springfield, MO: Gospel Publishing House.

————. 1966. *Temptations of the Spirit–Filled Christ.* Springfield, MO: Gospel Publishing House.

Geissler, Eugene S. 1973. *The Spirit Bible.* Notre Dame: Ave Maria Press.

Gentile, Ernest B. 1999. *Your Sons and Daughters Shall Prophesy.* Grand Rapids: Chosen Books.

Geraets, David. 1970. *Baptism of Suffering.* Pecos: Dove Publications.

Gillquist, Peter E. 1974. *Let's Quit Fighting About the Holy Spirit.* Grand Rapids: Zondervan.

Godet, Frederick Louis. 1893. *Commentary on the Gospel of John, Volume II.* Grand Rapids: Zondervan Publishing Company.

Goetchius, Eugene Van Ness. 1965. *The Language of the New Testament.* New York: Charles Scribner's Sons.

Goforth, Jonathan. 1942. *"By My Spirit".* Minneapolis: Bethany Fellowship.

Gordon, A.J. 1964. *The Ministry of the Spirit.* Minneapolis: Bethany Fellowship.

Graham, Billy. 1978. *The Holy Spirit.* Waco: Word Books.

Green, Joel B. 1997. *The Gospel of Luke.* Grand Rapids: Wm. B. Eerdmans.

Greenfield, John. 1967. *When the Spirit Came.* Minneapolis: Bethany Fellowship.

Gromacki, Robert G. 1974. *The Modern Tongues Movement.* Presbyterian and Reformed Publishing Company.

Gruber, Daniel C. 1991a. *My Heart's Desire*. Springfield: General Council of the Assemblies of God Intercultural Ministries Dept.

—————. 1991b. *The Church and the Jews*. Springfield: General Council of the Assemblies of God Intercultural Ministries Dept.

Grudem, Wayne A. 1982. *The Gift of Prophecy in 1 Corinthians*. Washington DC: University Press of America.

—————. 1988. *The Gift of Prophecy in the New Testament and Today*. Westchester: Crossway Books.

Guthrie, Donald. 1970. *New Testament Introduction*. London: The Tyndale Press.

Gutzke, Manford G. 1974. *Plain Talk about the Holy Spirit*. Grand Rapids: Baker Book House.

Haenchen, Ernst. 1971. *The Acts of the Apostles*. Philadelphia: The Westminster Press.

Hailey, Homer. 1981. *A Commentary on the Minor Prophets*. Grand Rapids: Baker Book House.

Halley, Henry H. 1951. *Pocket Bible Handbook*. Chicago: Henry H. Halley.

Harper, Michael. 1964a. *Power for the Body of Christ*. Plainfield: Logos Books.

—————. 1964b. *Prophecy: A Gift for the Body of Christ*. Plainfield: Logos Books.

—————. 1965. *As at the Beginning*. Plainfield: Logos International.

—————. 1966. *Life in the Holy Spirit*. Plainfield: Logos Books.

—————. 1968a. *The Baptism of Fire*. Plainfield: Logos Books.

—————. 1968b. *Walk in the Spirit*. Plainfield: Logos International.

Harrison, R. K. 1969. *Introduction to the Old Testament*. Grand Rapids: Wm. B. Eerdmans.

Hasel, Gerhard. 1972. *Old Testament Theology*. Grand Rapids: Wm. B. Eerdmans.

—————. 1978. *New Testament Theology*. Grand Rapids: Wm. B. Eerdmans.

Hawthorne, Gerald F. 1991. *The Presence and the Power*. Dallas: Word Publishing.

Hegre, T. A. 1960. *The Cross and Sanctification*. Minneapolis: Bethany Fellowship.

Hembree, Charles R. 1969. *Pocket of Pebbles*. Grand Rapids: Baker Book House.

Hendriksen, William. 1957. *New Testament Commentary: Exposition of the Pastoral Epistles*. Grand Rapids: Baker Book House.

—————. 1961. *New Testament Commentary. Exposition of the Gospel According to John.* Grand Rapids: Baker Book House.

—————. 1962. *New Testament Commentary. Exposition of Philippians.* Grand Rapids: Baker Book House.

—————. 1964. *New Testament Commentary. Exposition of Colossians and Philemon.* Grand Rapids: Baker Book House..

—————. 1967. *New Testament Commentary. Exposition of Ephesians.* Grand Rapids: Baker Book House..

—————. 1968. *New Testament Commentary: Exposition of Galatians.* Grand Rapids: Baker Book House.

Heron, Alasdaiaar I. C. 1983. *The Holy Spirit.* Philadelphia: The Westminster Press.

Heschel, Abraham J. 1962. *The Prophets,* Vol. II. New York: Harper & Row, Publishers.

Hildebrandt, Wilf. 1995. *An Old Testament Theology of the Spirit of God.* Peabody, MA: Hendrickson Publishers.

Hinson, E. Glenn. 1971. *The Broadman Bible Commentary, Vol. 11. 2 Corinthians–Philemon. 1–2 Timothy and Titus.* Nashville: Broadman Press.

Hodges, Melvin L. *Spiritual Gifts.* 1964. Springfield, MO: Gospel Publishing House.

Hoekema, Anthony A. 1972. *Holy Spirit Baptism.* Grand Rapids: Wm. B. Eerdmans.

Holdcroft, L. Thomas. 1971. *The Holy Spirit: A Pentecostal Interpretation.* North Vancouver: Pentecostal Bible College.

Horne, Charles M. 1971. *Salvation.* Chicago: Moody Press.

Horton, Harold. 1962. *The Gifts of the Spirit.* London: Assemblies of God Publishing House.

Horton, Stanley M. 1976. *What the Bible Says about the Holy Spirit.* Springfield, MO: Gospel Publishing House.

—————. 1981. *The Book of Acts.* Springfield, MO: Gospel Publishing House.

—————. 1991. *The Ultimate Victory.* Springfield, MO: Gospel Publishing House.

Howard, William F. n.d. *The Interpreter's Bible.* Abingdon Press.

Hubbard, David Allen. 1985. *Unwrapping Your Spiritual Gifts.* Waco: Word Books.

Hughes, Philip Edgcumbe. 1962. *The New International Commentary. Paul's Second Epistle to the Corinthians*. Grand Rapids: Wm. B. Eerdmans.

Hull, William E. 1970. *The Broadman Bible Commentary: Commentary on John*. Nashville: Broadman Press.

Hummel, Charles E. 1979. *Fire in the Fireplace: Contemporary Charismatic Renewal*. Downers Grove: Intervarsity Press.

————. 1981. *Filled with the Spirit*. Downers Grove: Inter–Varsity Press.

Hunter, Herold D. 1983. *Spirit–Baptism: A Pentecostal Alternative*. Lanham: University Press of America.

"In the Last Days…" (An Early History of the Assemblies of God)

James, Maynard. 1965. *I Believe in the Holy Spirit*. Minneapolis: Bethany Fellowship.

Jamieson, Robert, A. R. Faussett, and David Brown. 2003. *A Commentary, Critical and Explanatory, on the Old and New Testaments*. Electronic Database. Biblesoft, Inc.

Jensen, Richard A. 1975. *Touched by the Spirit*. Minneapolis: Augsburg Publishing House.

Johnson, Luke Timothy. 1999. *The Writings of the New Testament*. Minneapolis: Fortress Press.

Joseph, Léon. 1975. *A New Pentecost?* London: Darton, Longman, and Todd.

Kaiser, Walter C, Jr. 1978. *Toward an Old Testament Theology*. Grand Rapids: Zondervan.

————. 1981. *Toward an Exegetical Theology*. Grand Rapids: Baker Book House.

————. 1983. *Toward Old Testament Ethics*. Grand Rapids: Zondervan.

————. 1985. *The Uses of the Old Testament in the New*. Chicago: Moody Press.

————. 1987. *Toward Rediscovering The Old Testament*. Grand Rapids: Zondervan.

Keener, Craig S. 1993. *The IVP Bible Background Commentary*. Downer's Grove: InterVarsity Press.

————. 1997. *The Spirit in the Gospels and Acts*. Peabody, MA: Hendrickson Publishers.

————. 2001. *Gift and Giver: The Holy Spirit for Today*. Grand Rapids: Baker Academic.

—————. 2003. *The Gospel of John.* 2 Vols. Peabody, MA: Hendrickson Publishers.

Keil, Karl Friedrich, and Franz Delitzsch. 1969. *Commentary on the Old Testament.* 10 vols. Grand Rapids: Wm. B. Eerdmans.

Kelly, J. N. D. 1963. *A Commentary on the Pastoral Epistles.* Grand Rapids: Baker Book House.

Kendall, R. T. 1988. *God Meant It for Good.* Charlotte: Morning Star Publications.

—————. 2003. *The Anointing: Yesterday, Today, Tomorrow.* Lake Mary: Charisma House.

Kildahl, John P. 1972. *The Psychology of Speaking in Tongues.* New York: Harper and Row Publishers.

Kistemaker, Simon J. 1986. *Exposition of the Epistle of James and the Epistles of John: New Testament Commentary.* Grand Rapids: Baker Book House.

Kuyper, Abraham. 1900. *The Work of the Holy Spirit.* Grand Rapids: Wm. B. Eerdmans.

Kydd, Ronald A.N. 1984. *Charismatic Gifts in the Early Church.* Peabody, Hendrickson Publishers.

Ladd, George Eldon. 1959. *The Gospel of the Kingdom.* Grand Rapids: Wm. B. Eerdmans.

—————. 1972. *A Commentary on the Revelation of John.* Grand Rapids: Wm. B. Eerdmans.

—————. 1974. *A Theology of the New Testament.* Grand Rapids: Wm. B. Eerdmans.

Lampe, G. W. H. 1967. *The Seal of the Spirit.* London: SPCK.

—————. 1977. *God as Spirit.* Oxford: Clarendon Press.

Lederle, H. L. 1988. *Treasures New and Old.* Peabody, MA: Hendrickson Publishers.

Lenski, R. C. H. 1942. *St. John's Gospel.* Columbus: The Wartburg Press.

—————. 1945. *St. Paul's Epistle to the Romans.* Columbus: Wartburg Press.

—————. 1946a. *St. Luke's Gospel.* Columbus: The Wartburg Press.

—————. 1946b. *St. Paul's Epistles to the Galatians, Ephesians, and Philippians.* Columbus: The Wartburg Press.

—————. 1946c. *St. Paul's Epistles to the Colossians, to the Thessalonians, to Timothy, to Titus and to Philemon.* Columbus: The Wartburg Press.

————. 1946d. *St. Paul's First and Second Epistle to the Corinthians*. Columbus: Wartburg Press.

————. 1961. *The Acts of the Apostles*. Minneapolis: Augsburg Publishing House.

————. 1966a. *The Epistles of St. Peter, St. John, and St. Jude*. Minneapolis: Augsburg Publishing House.

————. 1966b. *The Epistle to the Hebrews and the Epistle of James*. Minneapolis: Augsburg Publishing House.

Lillie, D. G. 1966. *Tongues Under Fire*. Plainfield: Logos Books.

Lim, David. 1991. *Spiritual Gifts: A Fresh Look*. Springfield, MO: Gospel Publishing House.

Lloyd-Jones, Martyn. 1974. *Romans: The Sons of God*. Grand Rapids: Zondervan.

————. 1984. *Joy Unspeakable*. Wheaton: Harold Shaw Publishers.

————. 1997. *God the Holy Spirit*. Wheaton: Crossway Books.

Ma, Wonsuk. 1999. *Until the Spirit Comes: The Spirit of God in the Book of Isaiah*. Sheffield: Sheffield Academic Press.

Macchia, Frank D. 2006. *Baptized in the Spirit*. Grand Rapids: Zondervan.

MacDonald, William G. n.d. *Glossolalia in the New Testament*. Springfield, MO: Gospel Publishing House.

MacGorman, John William. 1971. *The Broadman Bible Commentary, Vol. 11. 2 Corinthians–Philemon. Galatians*. Nashville: Broadman Press.

————. 1974. *The Gifts of the Spirit*. Nashville: Broadman Press.

Machen, J. Gresham. 1951. *New Testament Greek for Beginners*. Toronto: The Macmillan Company.

Macpherson, Ian. 1970. *Like a Dove Descending*. Minneapolis: Bethany Fellowship.

————. 1972. *The Gift of Fire*. Minneapolis: Bethany Fellowship.

Maddux, Robert. 1982. *The Purpose of Luke–Acts*. Edinburgh: T & T Clark.

Mallone, George. 1983. *Those Controversial Gifts*. Downers Grove: InterVarsity Press.

Marsh, F. E. 1971. *Emblems of the Holy Spirit*. Grand Rapids: Kregel Publications.

Marshall, Alfred. 1960. *The Interlinear Greek–English New Testament*. London: Samuel Bagster and Sons Limited.

Marshall, I. Howard. 1978. *The Gospel of Luke*. Exeter: The Paternoster Press.

————. 1988. *Luke: Historian and Theologian*. Downers Grove: Intervarsity Press. Original copyright, 1970.

Martens, Elmer A. 1986. *God's Design*. Grand Rapids: Baker Book House.

Martin, Ralph P. 1971. *The Broadman Bible Commentary, Vol. 11. 2 Corinthians–Philemon. Ephesians*. Nashville: Broadman Press.

McDowell, Edward A. n.d. *Broadman Bible Commentary: Luke to John, Vol. 9*. ed. *Clifton J. Allen*. Nashville: Broadman Press.

————. n.d. *Broadman Bible Commentary: Hebrews to Revelation, Vol. 12*. ed. *Clifton J. Allen*. Nashville: Broadman Press.

McGee, Gary B., ed. 1991. *Initial Evidence*. Peabody, MA: Hendrickson Publishers.

Menzies, Robert P. 1994. *Empowered for Witness*. Sheffield: Sheffield Academic Press.

Menzies, William W., and Robert P. Menzies. 2000. *Spirit and Power*. Grand Rapids: Zondervan.

Miller, Elmer C. 1936. *Pentecost Examined*. Springfield, MO: Gospel Publishing House.

Mills, Watson. 1972. *Understanding Speaking in Tongues*. Grand Rapids: Wm. B. Eerdmans.

————. ed. 1973. *Speaking in Tongues: Let's Talk About It*. Waco: Word Books.

————. 1986. *Speaking in Tongues: A Guide to Research on Glossolalia*. Grand Rapids: Wm. B. Eerdmans.

Moltmann, Jürgen. 1992. *The Spirit of Life*. Minneapolis: Fortress Press.

Montague, George T. *1976. The Holy Spirit: Growth of a Biblical Tradition*. New York: Paulist Press.

Moody, Dale. 1970. *Romans. The Broadman Bible Commentary, Volume 10*. Nashville: Broadman Press.

Morgan, G. Campbell. 1953. *The Spirit of God*. Old Tappan: Fleming H. Revell Company.

Morris, Leon. 1959. *The First and Second Epistles to the Thessalonians*. Grand Rapids: Wm. B. Eerdmans.

————. 1971. *The Gospel According to John*. Grand Rapids: Wm. B. Eerdmans.

————. 1983. *The Atonement*. Downers Grove: Inter-Varsity Press.

————. 1986. *New Testament Theology*. Grand Rapids: Zondervan.

Moule, C. F. D. 1978. *The Holy Spirit*. London: Mowbray.

Mounce, Robert H. 1998. *The Book of Revelation*. Rev. ed. Grand Rapids: Wm. B. Eerdmans.

Mounce, William D. 2003. *Basics of Biblical Greek*. 2. ed. Grand Rapids: Zondervan.

Mülen, Heribert. 1978. *A Charismatic Theology: Initiation in the Spirit*. London: Burns and Oats.

Murray, Andrew. n.d. *The Spirit of Christ*. London: Nisbet and Co.

—————. n.d. *The Full Blessing of Pentecost*. Plainfield: Logos International.

—————. 1954. *The Full Blessing of Pentecost*. London: Lowe and Brydone.

Neve, Lloyd. 1972. *The Spirit of God in the Old Testament*. Tokyo: Seibunsha.

Nichol, John Thomas. 1966. *The Pentecostals*. Plainfield: Logos International.

Newport, John P. 1986. *The Lion and the Lamb*. Nashville: Broadman Press.

Oates, Wayne E. 1974. *The Holy Spirit and Contemporary Man*. Grand Rapids: Baker Book House.

O'Connor, Edward D. 1972. *Pentecost in the Modern World*. Notre Dame: Ave Maria Press.

Osborne, Grant. R. 1984. *The Resurrection Narratives*. Grand Rapids: Baker Book House.

Otis, George. 1970. '*You Shall Receive... '*. Van Nuys: Bible Voice.

Owen, John. 1954. *The Holy Spirit*. Grand Rapids: Kregel Publications.

Pache, Rene. 1957. *The Person and Work of the Holy Spirit*. Chicago: Moody Press.

Palma, Anthony D. 1974. *The Spirit—God in Action*. Springfield, MO: Gospel Publishing House.

—————. 1999. *Baptism in the Holy Spirit*. Springfield, MO: Gospel Publishing House.

Palmer, Edwin H. 1974. *The Person and Ministry of the Holy Spirit*. Grand Rapids: Baker Book House.

Payne, J. Barton. 1962. *The Theology of the Older Testament*. Grand Rapids: Zondervan.

Pentecost, J. Dwight. 1958. *Things to Come*. Findlay: Dunham Publishing Company.

—————. 1963. *The Divine Comforter*. Chicago: Moody Press.

————. 1990. *Thy Kingdom Come.* Wheaton: Victor Books.

Peterson, Douglas. 1996. *Not by Might nor by Power.* Carlisle: Regnum Books International.

Petts, David. 1998. *The Holy Spirit: An Introduction.* Mattersey: Mattersey Hall.

Pink, Arthur. 1970. *The Holy Spirit.* Grand Rapids: Baker Book House.

Pulkingham, Graham W. 1972. *Gathered for Power.* New York: Morehouse–Barlow.

Quy, Douglas S. 1973. *'Speaking the Truth in Love...'.* London: Penielpress.

Ramm, Bernard L. 1959. *The Witness of the Spirit.* Grand Rapids: Wm. B. Eerdmans.

————. 1974. *Rapping about the Spirit.* Waco: Word Books.

Rea, John. 1972. *Layman's Commentary on the Holy Spirit.* Plainfield: Logos International.

————. 1998. *Bible Handbook on the Holy Spirit.* Orlando: Creation House.

Ridderbos, Herman. 1962. *The Coming of the Kingdom.* Philadelphia: The Presbyterian and Reformed Publishing Company.

————. 1975. *Paul: An Outline of His Theology.* Grand Rapids: Wm. B. Eerdmans.

Riggs, Ralph M. 1949. *The Spirit Himself.* Springfield: Gospel Publishing House.

Robertson, A. T. 1930. *Word Pictures in the New Testament.* 6 Vols. Nashville: Broadman Press.

————. 1934. *A Grammar of the Greek New Testament in the Light of Historical Research.* Nashville: Broadman Press.

Robertson, O. Palmer. 1980. *The Christ of the Covenants.* Phillipsburg: Presbyterian and Reformed Publishing Company.

Rosato, Phillip J. 1981. *The Spirit As Lord.* Edinburgh: T & T Clark.

Ryken, Leland. 1984. *How to Read the Bible as Literature.* Grand Rapids: Academie Books.

————. 1992. *Words of Delight.* 2. ed. Grand Rapids: Baker Book House.

Ryrie, Charles Caldwell. 1959. *Biblical Theology of the New Testament.* Chicago: Moody Press.

Sanders, John. 1992. *No Other Name.* Grand Rapids: Wm. B. Eerdmans.

Schatzmann, Siegfried. 1987. *A Pauline Theology of Charismata.* Peabody, MA: Hendrickson Publishers.

Schep, John A. 1972. *Baptism in the Spirit*. Plainfield: Logos International.

Schlink, Basilea. 1969. *Ruled by the Spirit*. Minneapolis: Bethany Fellowship.

————. 1970. *When God Calls*. Minneapolis: Bethany Fellowship.

Schultz, Samuel J. 1970. *The Old Testament Speaks*. New York: Harper & Row, Publishers.

Schweizer, Eduard. 1980. *The Holy Spirit*. Philadelphia: Fortress Press.

Scroggie, W. Graham. 1948. *A Guide to the Gospels*. London: Pickering and Inglis Ltd.

Scofield, C. I. 19653. *Plain Papers on the Doctrine of the Holy Spirit*. Westwood: Fleming H. Revell Company.

Shank, Robert. 1960. *Life in the Son*. Springfield: Westcott Publishers.

Shelton, James B. 1991. *Mighty in Word and Deed*. Peabody, MA: Hendrickson Publishers.

Sigal, Phillip. 1988. *Judaism: The Evolution of a Faith*. Grand Rapids: Wm. B. Eerdmans.

Simpson, A. B. 1896. *The Holy Spirit*. 2 Vols. Harrisburg: Christian Publications.

Skinner, J. 1951. *The Book of the Prophet Isaiah*. Cambridge: The University Press.

Spittler, Russell P., ed. 1976. *Perspectives on the New Pentecostalism*. Grand Rapids: Baker Book House.

Stagg, Frank. 1971. *The Broadman Bible Commentary, Vol. 11. Philippians*. Nashville: Broadman Press.

Stamm, Raymond T. 1953. *The Interpreter's Bible. The Epistle to the Galatians*. New York: Abingdon Press.

Stibbs, A. M., and J. I. Packer. 1967. *The Spirit Within You*. London: Hodder and Stoughton.

Stott, John R. W. 1964a. *Baptism and Fullness*. Leicester: Inter–Varsity Press.

————. 1964b. *The Baptism and Fullness of the Holy Spirit*. Downers Grove: Inter–Varsity Press.

————. 1972. *The Baptism and Fullness of the Holy Spirit*. Downers Grove: Inter–Varsity Press.

Strauss, Lehman. 1954. *The Third Person*. New York: Loizeaux Brothers.

Stronstad, Roger. 1984. *The Charismatic Theology of St. Luke*. Peabody, MA: Hendrickson Publishers.

—————. 1995. *Spirit, Scripture, and Theology: A Pentecostal Perspective.* Baguio City: Asia Pacific Theological Seminary Press.

Sullivan, Francis A. 1982. *Charisms and Charismatic Renewal.* Ann Arbor: Servant Books.

Swete, Henry Barclay. 1910. *The Holy Spirit in the New Testament.* London: Macmillan and Company.

Synan, Vinson. 1971. *The Holiness–Pentecostal Movement.* Grand Rapids: Wm. B. Eerdmans.

Tasker, R. V. G. *The Gospel According to John.* Grand Rapids: Wm. B. Eerdmans.

Terrien, Samuel. 1978. *The Elusive Presence.* San Francisco: Harper and Row Publishers.

Teuber, Andrew S. 1966. *Tongues of Fire.* Springfield.

Thayer, Joseph Henry. 1962. *Greek–English Lexicon of the New Testament.* Grand Rapids: Zondervan.

Thiessen, Henry C. 1979. *Lectures in Systematic Theology.* Grand Rapids: Wm. B. Eerdmans.

Thomas, W. H. Griffith. 1964. *The Holy Spirit of God.* Grand Rapids: Wm. B. Eerdmans.

Torrey, R. A. n.d. *The Baptism with the Holy Spirit.* Minneapolis: Bethany Fellowship.

—————. n.d. *How to Find Fullness of Power.* Minneapolis: Bethany Fellowship.

—————. 1910. *The Person and Work of the Holy Spirit.* Grand Rapids: Zondervan.

—————. 1927. *The Holy Spirit: Who He Is and What He Does.* Westwood: Fleming H. Revell Company.

—————. 1972. *The Baptism with the Holy Spirit.* Minneapolis: Bethany Fellowship.

Tozer, A. W. n.d. *How to be Filled with the Holy Spirit.* Harrisburg: Christian Publications.

Turner, Max. 1996a. *Power from on High.* Sheffield: Sheffield Academic Press.

—————. 1996b. *The Holy Spirit and Spiritual Gifts.* Peabody, MA: Hendrickson Publishers.

Unger, Merrill F. 1974. *The Baptism and Gifts of the Holy Spirit.* Chicago: Moody Press.

—————. 1988. *The New Unger's Bible Dictionary.* Chicago: Moody Press.

VanGemeren, Willem. 1988. *The Progress of Redemption*. Grand Raids: Zondervan.

Von Rad, Gerhard. 1962. *Old Testament Theology, Volume 1*. New York: Harper and Row Publishers.

————. 1965. *Old Testament Theology, Volume 2*. New York: Harper and Row Publishers.

Wagner, C. Peter. 1979. *Your Spiritual Gifs*. Ventura: Regal Books.

Wainwright, Arthur W. 1962. *The Trinity in the New Testament*. London: SPCK.

Wallace, Daniel B. 1996. *Greek Grammar Beyond the Basics*. Grand Rapids: Zondervan.

Walvoord, John F. 1954. *The Holy Spirit*. Grand Rapids: Zondervan.

————. 1966. *The Revelation of Jesus Christ*. Chicago: Moody Press.

————. 1969. *Jesus Christ Our Lord*. Chicago: Moody Press.

Warfield, B. B. 1972. *Counterfeit Miracles*. London: Hazell Watson and Viney.

Wenham, J. W. 1965. *The Elements of New Testament Greek*. Cambridge University Press.

Westcott, B. F. *The Epistle to the Hebrews*. Nashville: Broadman Press,

————. 1971a. *The Epistles of St. John*. Grand Rapids: Wm. B. Eerdmans.

————. 1971b. *The Gospel According to St. John*. Grand Rapids: Wm. B. Eerdmans.

Williams, Ernest S. 1953. *Systematic Theology, Vol. III*. Springfield, MO: Gospel Publishing House.

Williams, J. Rodman. 1971. *The Era of the Spirit*. Plainfield: Logos International.

————. 1972. *The Pentecostal Reality*. Plainfield: Logos International.

Wilson, Ernest T. 1978. *The Messianic Psalms*. Neptune: Loizeaux Brothers.

Wilson, Everett A. 1997. *Strategy of the Spirit*. Carlisle: Regnum.

Wood, George O. 1996. *Acts: A Study Guide*. 2. ed. Springfield: ICI Press.

Wood, Laurence W. 1980. *Pentecostal Grace*. Wilmore, KY: Asbury Publishing Company.

Wood, Leon J. 1976. *The Holy Spirit in the Old Testament*. Grand Rapids: Zondervan.

————. 1979. *The Prophets of Israel*. Grand Rapids: Baker Book House.

Yates, Kyle M. 1942. *Preaching from the Prophets*. Nashville: Broadman Press.

Young, Edward J. 1952. *My Servants the Prophets*. Grand Rapids: Wm. B. Eerdmans.

————. 1972. *The Book of Isaiah*: Vol. 3, Chapters 40 through 66. Grand Rapids: Wm. B. Eerdmans.

————. 1984. *The Book of Isaiah, Volume 3*. Grand Rapids: Wm. B. Eerdmans.

Zuck, Roy B. 1963. *The Holy Spirit in Your Teaching*. Wheaton: Scripture Press Publications.

————, ed. 1991. *A Biblical Theology of the Old Testament*. Chicago: Moody Press.

ARTICLES

Fee, Gordon. D. 1977. "Once More—John 7:37–39." *Expository Times* 89 (1977–1978):116–118.

UNPUBLISHED DOCUMENTS

Flattery, Mark D. 2001. "A Contemporary Strategy for Church Growth Based on Principles from the Book of Acts." Unpublished Doctor of Ministry Thesis, Fuller Theological Seminary.

General Presbytery of the General Council of the Assemblies of God. 2000. "The Baptism in the Holy Spirit: The Initial Experience and Continuing Evidence of the Spirit–filled Life." August 11.

Higgins, John Robert. 1973. "The Relationship between Classic Pentecostalism and Neo–Pentecostalism." Unpublished Master of Theology Theses, Eastern Baptist Theological Seminary.

Ma, Wonsuk. 1996. "The Spirit of God in the Book of Isaiah and Its Eschatological Significance." Unpublished Doctor of Philosophy Thesis, Asia Pacific Theological Seminary.

Palma, Anthony David. 1966. "Tongues and Prophecy—A Comparative Study in Charismata." Unpublished Master of Sacred Theology Thesis, Concordia Seminary.

————. 1974. "The Holy Spirit in the Corporate Life of the Pauline Congregation." Unpublished Doctor of Theology Thesis, Concordia Seminary.

Parratt, John King. 1965. "The Seal of the Spirit in the New Testament." Unpublished Ph.D. Thesis, University of London.

Pretlove, John L. 1980. "Baptism *En Pneumati*: A Comparison of the Theologies of Luke and Paul." Unpublished Ph.D. Dissertation, Southwestern Baptist Theological Seminary

Smeeton, Donald D. 1971. "Perfection or Pentecost." Unpublished Master of Arts Thesis, Trinity Evangelical Divinity School.

Turner, Martin Maximillian Barnaby. 1980. "Luke and the Spirit." Unpublished Doctor of Philosophy Dissertation, University of Cambridge.

www.ingramcontent.com/pod-product-compliance
Lightning Source LLC
LaVergne TN
LVHW021450080426
835509LV00018B/2226